DoBrilliantly

A2 General Studies

Exam practice at its **best**

- **David Walton**
- **Trevor Green**
- **Series Editor: Jayne de Courcy**

Contents

Published by HarperCollins*Publishers* Ltd
77–85 Fulham Palace Road
London W6 8JB

www.**Collins**Education.com
On-line support for schools and colleges

© HarperCollins*Publishers* Ltd 2003

First published 2003

ISBN 0 00 716707 5

British Library Cataloguing in Publication Data
A catalogue record for this book is available from the British Library.

Edited by Margaret Shepherd
Production by Katie Butler
Book design by Bob Vickers
Printed and bound by Printing Express, Hong Kong

Acknowledgements
The Authors and Publishers are grateful to the following for permission to reproduce copyright material:
OCR pp. 38, 39, 44, 45, 56 (Q.3), 68, 69, 70
Edexcel pp. 13, 16, 25, 26, 27, 31, 32, 33, 46 (Q.2), 49 (Q.1), 50, 52
AQA pp. 8, 9, 17, 18, 19, 20, 22, 23, 24, 34, 35, 36, 40, 41, 47, 49 (Q.2), 54, 56 (Q.1 & 2), 57, 58, 62, 63, 64, 65, 71, 72, 73, 74, 75, 77, 78, 79, 80, 81, 82, 83, 84, 85, 88, 89, 90, 91
Answers to questions taken from past examination papers are entirely the responsibility of the Authors.

Every effort has been made to contact the holders of copyright material, but if any have been inadvertently overlooked, the Publishers will be pleased to make the necessary arrangements at the first opportunity.

You might also like to visit:
www.**fire**and**water**.com
The book lover's website

How this book will help you
by David Walton and Trevor Green

Key focus – Exam skills and technique

This book will **help you to improve your performance in A2 General Studies**, whichever specification you are following. It is not so much concerned with the knowledge you require – this will be covered in your course – it is about the **skills** you will be called upon to demonstrate in the exam.

There are **four different specifications** set by the three main boards and these are **AQA A, AQA B, Edexcel** and **OCR**. The exams are different in a number of ways, but the content and question styles overlap. **General Studies exams are mainly about skills** and, as **the Assessment Objectives are common for all specifications** (see page 6), it is the same sets of skills which are being assessed, even though some of the question types, or just the emphasis, may differ (see pages 4–5). Practising these key exam skills is what the book is all about.

Three main sections to this book

There are three main sections, which relate to the broad types of questions you will meet: source-based questions, essay questions and multiple choice questions (AQA A only). The questions are drawn from the range of **main topic areas** for A2 General Studies, which are:

- Culture, Morality, Arts and Humanities
- Science, Mathematics and Technology
- Society, Politics and the Economy.

The titles of the test units vary these combinations for Edexcel and OCR (see page 5) and in AQA B they look very different, but each specification covers the same basic range of topics **across the three A2 units**. In AQA B the topics are tested **in each unit** under the sub-headings of *Arts and Media, Beliefs and Values, Industry and Commerce, Science and Technology, Society and Politics*.

Questions for all specifications

We make clear what aspect or skill each question is designed to test, as set out in the question type grid on page 4. Some of the questions test more than one skill and this is shown alongside each question. **Using the grid, you can easily find and use the questions relevant to your particular specification**. Even though some of the question styles may be slightly different from the ones you have to answer, it is still worth working through these, as they are broadly testing the same basic skills, knowledge and understanding.

Examination questions, Students' answers and 'How to score full marks'

The first part of each chapter consists of typical questions followed by students' answers, **examiner's comments on strengths and weaknesses** and a section, **'How to score full marks'**. Look out for the **'Don't forget …'** boxes that summarise important aspects of exam technique.

Questions to try, Model answers and Examiner's comments

The second part of each chapter contains questions for you to answer. At the end of the book you will find model answers to each of the questions. These are answers that would score full marks, which you can compare against your own answers. We have provided comments on why these are particularly good answers.

Question types and exam skills

Question type number in this book	Description of question type/exam skill	AQA A units	AQA B units	Edexcel units	OCR units	Page numbers in this book
	Using sources: text, data and images					
1	Identifying and commenting on main points	6	4, 5, 6	4, 5	5, 6	9, 12, 58, 62–63
2	Analysing and commenting on data	6	6	5		13, 16
3	Analysing and summarising key points from data	6	4, 6			20, 24, 58, 62–63
4	Analysing knowledge and arguments	6	4, 5, 6	4, 5	5, 6	27, 33, 36, 39
5	Comparing different sources	6	6	4, 5	5, 6	20, 24, 27, 45
6	Developing ideas and arguments	6	5, 6	4, 5	5, 6	20, 24, 33, 36, 39, 45, 58, 62–63, 64–65, 68–70
7	Assessing validity and value	6	4, 6	4, 5	5, 6	36, 39
8	Summarising and evaluating key issues	6	4, 5, 6	4, 5	5, 6	41, 45, 58, 62–63, 64–65, 68–70
9	Drawing conclusions/discussing solutions	6	4, 6	4, 5	5, 6	20, 41, 45, 58, 62–63, 64–65, 68–70
	Essay questions					
10	Short answer/mini essay	6	5	4		46, 47, 49
11	Full essay	4, 5, 6	6	4, 5, 6	4, 5, 6	50, 52, 54, 56, 64–65, 68–70
12	Report writing		4			58, 62–63
13	**Foreign language comprehension (multiple choice)**	4				71–75, 77–80
14	**Mechanical and spatial relations (multiple choice)**	5				81–85, 88–91

What each Unit exam consists of

Specification	Unit 4	Unit 5	Unit 6 (Synoptic)
AQA A	**Culture, Morality, Arts and Humanities**	**Science, Mathematics and Technology**	**Society, Politics and the Economy**
	25 Multiple choice questions on Foreign language comprehension (French, German **or** Spanish) + Essay (one from choice of six) 1½ hours	25 Multiple choice questions on Mechanical and spatial relations + Essay (one from choice of six) 1½ hours	Four extended writing questions on pre-release Case Study documents + Essay (one from choice of four) 1½ hours
AQA B	**Conflict–Resolution**	**Power–Regulation**	**Space–Time**
	Structured report on problem solving exercise 1 hour	Five extended writing questions based on short stimulus material 1¼ hours	Two essays based on analysis and comparison of sources (one compulsory; one from choice of two) 1¾ hours
Edexcel	**Cultural Expressions**	**Modern Society**	**The Contemporary World**
	Three short answer questions + Comprehension: analysis of arguments + Essay (one from choice of three) 1½ hours	Data analysis (short answer questions) + Comprehension: analysis of arguments + Essay (one from choice of four) 1½ hours	Two essays based on analysis and comparison of sources (one compulsory; one from choice of two) 1¾ hours
OCR	**The Scientific and Cultural Domains**	**The Social Domain 2**	**Culture, Science and Society**
	Essay on scientific topic (one from choice of three) + Essay on cultural topic (one from choice of three) 1½ hours	Analysis, summary and commentary on source documents + Essay on social topic (one from choice of three) 1½ hours	Two essays based on analysis and commentary on contrasting sources 1½ hours

Make sure you know which specification you are following and exactly what you will have to do in each of the Unit tests. Then check the different question types for your Units on page 4.

Assessment objectives

This shows you what knowledge, understanding and skills are being assessed in A2 General Studies and their relative importance in terms of marks:

AO1   Demonstrate relevant knowledge and understanding applied to a range of issues, using skills from different disciplines (20–30%)

AO2   Communicate clearly and accurately in a concise, logical and relevant way (10–15%)

AO3   Marshal evidence and draw conclusions; select, interpret, evaluate and integrate information, data, concepts and opinions (35–45%)

AO4   Demonstrate understanding of different types of knowledge and of the relationship between them, appreciating their limitations (20–30%)

Note on AO2

This assesses the quality of your written communication and in particular your ability to:

- select and use a form and style of writing appropriate to the question's purpose and subject matter
- organise relevant information clearly and coherently, using appropriate vocabulary
- ensure text is legible and spelling, grammar and punctuation are accurate, so that the meaning is clear.

Note on AO4

This is a new element in General Studies specifications. In the past, there has been a focus on the knowledge of facts (AO1), and the marshalling of evidence (AO3) – on what might be called 'first-order' knowledge. This is still fundamental; but AO4 is about understanding **what counts as knowledge**; about how far knowledge is based upon facts and values; and about standards of proof.

By 'different types of knowledge' we mean *different ways of getting knowledge*. We might obtain knowledge by fine measurement, and calculation. This gives us a degree of **certainty**. We might obtain it by observation, and by experiment. This gives us a degree of **probability**. Or we might obtain it by examination of documents and material remains, or by introspection – that is, by canvassing our own experiences and feelings. This gives us a degree of **possibility**. In this sense, knowledge is a matter of degree.

Questions that are designed to test AO4 will focus on such things as:

- analysis and evaluation of the **nature of the knowledge**, evidence or arguments, for example, used in a text, set of data or other form of stimulus material;
- understanding of the crucial **differences between knowledge, belief or opinion**, and objectivity and subjectivity in arguments;
- appreciation of **what constitutes proof**, cause and effect, truth, validity, justification, and the **limits** to these;
- recognition of the **existence of personal values**, value judgements, partiality and bias in given circumstances;
- awareness of the effects upon ourselves and others of different phenomena, such as the **nature of physical, emotional and spiritual experiences**, and the ability to draw upon and analyse first-hand knowledge and understanding of these.

All the material and questions in Part A Chapters 3–6 and Part B Chapters 2–4 test aspects of this assessment objective.

Synoptic Units in A2 General Studies

In A2 General Studies each exam board's **Unit 6** is called the Synoptic Unit. This is the Unit that is designed to bring together **all the main skills** of General Studies and knowledge and understanding from **different disciplines and subjects**. The topics and questions (mostly essays) are broad and will often require you to bring together your knowledge and understanding about the arts, humanities, sciences and social sciences, morals and ethics **in single questions.** Typically they are about 'big' themes and issues that affect contemporary society and there are plenty of typical examples of these questions on pages 8–9, 11–12, 17–20, 22–24, 34–36, 38–39, 52, 64–65 and 68–70.

Preparing for the AQA A Unit 6 Case Study

This test is a little different from the other boards' Unit 6 tests as it is based on pre-released material issued to you several weeks in advance of the exam. This is to allow time for you to think about and improve your understanding of the topic and the issues raised in preparation for questions in the exam.

The material will always be substantial and will require **several hours of preparation** – the board recommends **at least 3 hours**. Typically there will be a collection of five or six different extracts from newspapers (usually broadsheet, but not always) and other sources:

- They will be based on broad themes specified for the module, e.g. The Family, Transport, Globalisation, Crime and Punishment.
- They will be drawn from a variety of disciplines (including statistics and tables of data) representing different aspects, viewpoints and issues relevant to the topic.

In the test itself, the questions will require you to:
- show your **understanding of the detail** of the material
- be able to **summarise** the points and arguments contained within the extracts
- recognise the **connections** between the different elements of the subject
- identify different **standpoints and values** represented
- exercise your **own judgements and knowledge** on the nature of the arguments and problems.

Questions relating to statistical data will test your:
- appreciation of their **use in the context** of a broader set of issues
- understanding of what they reveal in terms of **support for arguments** presented
- evaluation of **implications and conclusions** that may be drawn.

Solid preparation of this material is therefore vital, as the questions will require your understanding of the **detail** as well as broader understanding of the **issues**. In your preparation you should:
- ensure that you understand key **vocabulary, terms and concepts**
- summarise for yourself, and in your own words, the **main themes and arguments**
- draw **points** together **from the different extracts**
- make **connections and comparisons** between them
- analyse the data to establish **what they reveal** in their own right
- consider the extent to which they **support** ideas and arguments presented in the extracts
- evaluate the contribution each makes to **the larger picture.**

1 IDENTIFYING AND COMMENTING ON THE MAIN POINTS

Identifying the main points in a source is central to all exam work with sources whichever General Studies specification you are taking at A2. You can apply the techniques in this chapter to any source-based questions you have to answer. Developing an overview of points, arguments and issues is vital to your comprehension of sources and will help you answer broader and more demanding questions.

QUESTION AND STUDENT'S ANSWER

Source 1: EXTRACT FROM THE GOVERNMENT'S WHITE PAPER ON TRANSPORT

We want a transport system that is safe, efficient, clean and fair. We need a new approach, bringing together the public and private sectors in a partnership which benefits everyone. We want to ensure that companies have incentives to provide new services and raise standards, that taxpayers' money is spent wisely to make public transport available for all and that services are properly regulated in the public interest.

The way forward is through an integrated transport policy. This means integration:

- within and between different types of transport, so each works properly and people can make easy connections between them;
- with the environment, so that our transport choices cause less damage;
- with land use planning, to support more sustainable travel choices;
- with our policies for education, health and wealth creation, so that transport helps to make a fairer, more inclusive society.

An integrated transport system is not just an aspiration. There are already some successful local initiatives which point the way – against the grain of national trends over the last twenty years. What has been lacking is strategic direction and support, and this is what our New Deal will supply, starting with the way we plan.

The key to integration is to plan for it locally as well as nationally, which is why we are introducing *local transport plans* as a core part of our proposals. Local authorities will set out their strategies for transport and their long-term targets, for instance for improving air quality, road safety and public transport and for reducing road traffic.

They will have new tools, including road user charging and levies on workplace parking, to tackle congestion and pollution. The money raised will help fund other transport improvements. These new powers must be used as part of clear transport strategies which have the backing of local communities.

We will also revise the planning guidance to local councils to improve town and country planning and reduce reliance on the car. A good example is the new Millennium urban village in Greenwich, designed so that local services are within walking distance and public transport links are convenient.

Source: DETR July 1998

Question type 1

Identify **three** of the main aims of the Government's proposals on Transport and assess how appropriate they are as a means of solving Britain's transport problems. [6 marks]

AMY'S ANSWER

In the Government's White Paper of 1998 integration was cited as one of the main aims of Transport policy. Integration includes integrating between different types of transport, which is immediately a problem. There are vested interests in different transport sectors, i.e. buses and trains, signals fragmentation and companies working for themselves competitively rather than in the interests of the public. As has been seen with the privatisation of the railways, cooperation between different companies doesn't work.

The Government also expresses a desire to plan locally. This it seems is a well thought out and appropriate idea. It appears as though the government are afraid of acting nationally and seem to frequently bow to commercial pressure. However, if local authorities set out the strategies that will work best for their particular area they will be backed by their local communities. A good example is Greenwich where such a scheme has worked.

Thirdly, the Government plans to introduce road user charging and levies on workplace parking. This is not a good idea as it will be very unpopular and probably lose them the next election. Running a car costs enough as it is without having to pay extra. This may suit people with company cars but what about poor people and those who live out in the country where there is no public transport? They won't be able to afford to run a car anymore.

4/6

Integration is one of the government's main aims, and Amy's comment is valid, even though the intention is to overcome the problems of fragmentation through better integration of services.

This is a well-supported point giving both a valid reason and an illustration.

Although it is mentioned in the source, this is not a main aim. It is a measure that a local authority might take to achieve broader aims of reducing congestion.

How to score full marks

It should be fairly obvious with this question that there are **3 marks for identifying** each of three main aims from the source and **another 3 for supporting** assessments, i.e. 2 for each set of points. Amy has identified two aims correctly and given a reasoned view of their appropriateness in each case.

The third paragraph cannot count as an aim. Aims are **broad intentions**. There are quite a few to choose from in the source, and the same sentence that mentions road charging refers to tackling congestion and pollution. These are the **aims**; road charging and workplace levies are **measures** through which reducing congestion and pollution might be achieved. At this level your **interpretation has to be precise**.

On short answer questions carrying not many marks such as this, it pays to **be concise**. 'Identify' means **merely point out**. A phrase or sentence will do for this part of the answer. e.g.

- 'A transport system that is safe, efficient, clean and fair' from the first sentence could represent four aims in itself, if each were developed successfully.
- 'An integrated transport policy' in the second paragraph again involves four distinct possibilities, shown as bullet points, each of which could be developed as well.
- Other broad aims mentioned in the source include 'improving air quality, road safety, public transport and reducing road traffic', or 'tackling congestion and pollution'.

For the second part of the answer an appropriate supporting argument is all that is required. **A single sentence** can do this. There are points where Amy says too much and almost spoils her argument, e.g. the final sentence of her first paragraph and the third sentence of her second paragraph do not effectively serve the purpose of the question. They are **not needed to score the limited number of marks available** and her answer would be better without them.

The key skill for this type of question is **identifying main points** in a source. Two valid points reasonably supported give Amy 4 out 6 marks.

Don't forget ...

If you are a candidate for **AQA Specification A Unit 6** this involves a varied selection of source documents similar to the ones used throughout this book, issued as pre-release material up to 8 weeks before the exam. General advice about how to prepare for this is set out on page 7. **Identifying the main points** in each of the documents is a vital part of your preparation.

One **essential aspect** of working with sources is using your judgment about what are the key points being made. They often come (in 70% of cases) in the **first sentence of a new paragraph**. Before you can make the necessary judgements you have to **read the whole passage** to work out what it is essentially about. The **title** will sometimes give you a clue as well.

Source 2: GOVERNMENT POLICY ON CRIME

Her Majesty The Queen has outlined the Government's plans for the year ahead at the State Opening of Parliament. At the heart of the Government's legislative programme is a commitment to reform and rebalance the criminal justice system to deliver justice and to safeguard the interests of victims, witnesses and communities.

The crime reduction elements are as follows:

- The Government will introduce a Bill to tackle anti-social behaviour, intended to make it easier to evict anti-social tenants. The use of fixed penalty notices will be extended and the number of people enforcing them increased. Measures will be introduced to tackle graffiti, use of spray paints, fly-tipping, vandalism and dangerous use of airguns, and fireworks.

- A Bill will be introduced to reform sentencing arrangements and criminal procedures. Sentencing will be reformed to ensure that the punishment is appropriate for the offender. New types of sentence will be introduced to protect the public from dangerous offenders, help reduce re-offending and deal with young offenders. The Bill will also allow retrials for those acquitted of serious offences where new and compelling evidence emerges. It will also simplify the rules of evidence to allow judge and jury to hear all the facts, including relevant previous convictions of a defendant.

- Legislation will also be introduced to reform the courts system. It will bring together Magistrates' Courts and the Crown Court to work more effectively under a single organisation. New sanctions will allow courts to enforce the payment of fines more efficiently.

- A Bill will be brought forward to modernise the laws on sexual offences and to strengthen the framework of penalties for sex offenders to protect the public. The bill will crackdown on paedophiles using the Internet. It will strengthen the Sex Offenders' Register by tightening notification requirements and broadening offences that trigger registration.

- A Bill will also be introduced to improve international co-operation in tackling crime, including drugs trafficking, and to modernise the arrangements for international mutual assistance to catch criminals.

- The Government will bring forward legislation to streamline the licensing system for premises selling alcohol. This will abolish fixed opening hours and introduce a range of measures to reduce anti-social behaviour.

Source: Crime Reduction Elements of the Queen's Speech 2003
www.crimereduction.gov.uk/legislation22.htm

Question type 1

(a) Identify the two main aims of the Government's proposals on Crime for 2003.   [2 marks]

(b) Identify four of the measures that the Government is planning to introduce and indicate what each is intended to do.   [4 marks]

Examiner's hints
- Note that you are not required in this question to give your opinion on the issues involved.
- Always tailor your answer to the precise question set and write no more than is necessary for the number of marks involved.
- A single sentence or two phrases is all that is required for (a) and four phrases each followed by a single sentence for (b).

Answers can be found on page 92.

2 ANALYSING AND COMMENTING ON DATA

Questions that require you to analyse and comment on data can appear in any of the General Studies specifications at A2. The short answer questions in this chapter are useful preparation for any specification. They practise the simple techniques you need to apply to data to make sense of them and the trends that they show. They are also useful to work through because of the background knowledge and issues that they raise.

QUESTION AND STUDENT'S ANSWER

Source 3: WHO BENEFITS FROM YOUR TAX?

How Labour and Conservative tax spending priorities compare

	Labour 2001	Conservative 1996
Total spending	**£394bn**	**£315bn**
Debt interest	6%	8%
Defence	6%	7%
Education	13%	12%
Health	18%	17%
Housing and environment	4%	5%
Industry, agriculture and employment	4%	4%
Law and order	6%	5%
Other[1]	12%	7%
Social security	28%	32%
Transport	3%	3%

[1] includes Culture, media and sport; International cooperation and development; and Public service pensions

Source: *The Sunday Times* 11 March 2001

Question type 2

(a) By calculation, show that the
  (i) change in actual expenditure on education is £13.42 billion   [1 mark]
  (ii) percentage change in actual expenditure on social security is 9.44%.   [1 mark]

(b) Comment on the reasons for **each** of these changes.   [4 marks]

[Total 6 marks]

ANDY'S ANSWER

(a) (i)

13% of 394 = 51.22

12% of 315 = 37.80

51.22 − 37.80 = 13.42

Actual difference in expenditure = £13.42bn

✓

(ii)

28% of 394 = 110.32

32% of 315 = 100.80

110.32 − 100.80 = 9.52

Difference = 9.52% ?

✗

(b) A possible reason for the increase in expenditure on education is that when the Labour government came to power it promised to spend more on education. Tony Blair said 'education, education, education' was the government's priority.

✓

Another reason why expenditure has increased on both education and social security could be because of inflation. The cost of everything has gone up.

✓

Total ③/6

How to score full marks

Andy uses the correct procedure and calculation for **(a) (i)**, but fails to complete the extra step needed for **(a) (ii)**. The second part requires you to calculate the **percentage change**, which means the percentage difference between the actual figures for 1996 and 2001.

To calculate this, use the 1996 figure of £100.80bn as the base, work out the difference between this and the 2001 figure (110.32 − 100.80 = 9.52) and then calculate the difference as a **percentage of the base figure** to give the percentage change (9.52/100.80 × 100 = 9.44%).

For part **(b)** Andy's points are acceptable but rather vague and hypothetical. For full marks a **more definite and detailed** answer was needed based on some knowledge of recent government policy and current affairs. He would have gained extra marks for any of the following points:

Education

- improved performance-related pay for teachers
- reduction of primary class sizes
- increased examination costs
- expansion of further and higher education

Social security

- reduction in unemployment
- clamp down on benefit fraud
- increases in pensions and child benefit
- introduction of working families tax credit

Some **points on both** were needed for full marks.

Don't forget ...

An **actual change** is different from a **percentage change**, and you need to take extra care when you are dealing with percentage figures or changes in proportions, e.g. as in **(a) (ii)** and in the Question to Try which follows. A **decrease in proportion** can still mean a **percentage increase**.

Some **background knowledge** is required for the second part of these questions. You should get this from the course you are following or from newspaper reading of current affairs. Look out for **statistical data** and **commentaries** on trends that are published by the government from time to time and covered in the press. A good source is an annual publication called *Social Trends*, which you will find in your local library.

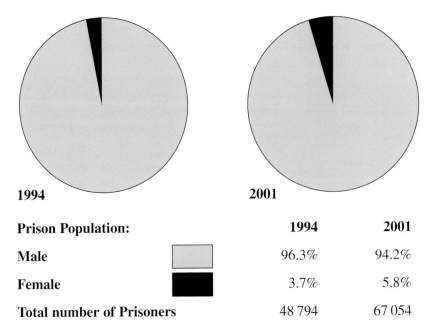

Source 4: PRISON POPULATIONS IN 1994 AND 2001

1994   2001

Prison Population:		**1994**	**2001**
Male		96.3%	94.2%
Female		3.7%	5.8%
Total number of Prisoners		48 794	67 054

Source: Prison Service
© Crown Copyright 2001

Question type 2

(a) Calculate

   (i) the change between 1994 and 2001 in the number of female prisoners   [1 mark]

   (ii) the percentage increase between 1994 and 2001 in the number of male prisoners.   [1 mark]

(b) What factors might explain the changes in the prison population?   [4 marks]

[Total 6 marks]

Examiner's hints
- The calculation processes for **(a) (i)** and **(ii)** are very similar to the question on government expenditure in Source 3. Note that **(a) (ii)** is asking for the percentage increase in the **number** of male prisoners, not the change in proportion.
- Note also that the wording of **(b)** allows a more hypothetical or speculative response. However, like the previous question, you need to comment on both the changes to male and female populations for full marks.

Answers can be found on pages 92–93.

3 ANALYSING AND SUMMARISING KEY POINTS FROM DATA

Each examining group is required to set a Synoptic Unit at A2, designed to bring together knowledge and skills from different study areas. The questions in these Units are much broader than in other Units (see page 7 for more about the Synoptic Unit).

The questions in this chapter are about bringing knowledge and understanding together from the different charts and tables, and recognising the relationship between them and the issues which they present.

The AQA Unit 6 Case Study is issued in advance of the test, so that you have plenty of time to study the data and information before sitting the examination (see page 7).

QUESTION AND STUDENT'S ANSWER

Source 5: CHANGES IN THE FAMILY

Data on households and families

In 1998 the population of the United Kingdom was estimated to be 59.2 million. In 1901 it was 38.2 million. Over the same period the number of households increased from approximately 8.3 million to an estimated 24.6 million. In 1901 about 1 in 20 households comprised one person living alone; this increased to just under one in three in 1998–99.

For many decades censuses did not distinguish adequately between households and families, and a definitive distinction was not made until 1961. A household is defined as one person living alone, or a group of people at the same address who share living arrangements. Families are defined as a married or cohabiting couple with or without their never-married children who have no children of their own, or a lone parent with such children. Most household surveys do not consider a person living alone to form a family. A household can contain one or more families and also members other than those belonging to a nuclear family.

Chart 1

Households: by type of household and family Percentages

	1961	1971	1981	1991	1998–99
One person					
Under pensionable age	4	6	8	11	14
Over pensionable age	7	12	14	16	15
Two or more unrelated adults	5	4	5	3	2
One-family households					
Couple					
No children	26	27	26	28	30
1–2 dependent children	30	26	25	20	19
3 or more dependent children	8	9	6	5	4
Non-dependent children only	10	8	8	8	6
Lone parent					
Dependent children	2	3	5	6	7
Non-dependent children only	4	4	4	4	3
Multi-family households	3	1	1	1	1
All households					
(millions) (= 100%)	16.3	18.6	20.2	22.4	...

Chart 2
Marriages and divorces

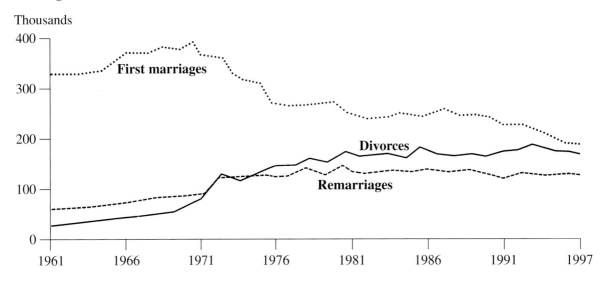

Thousands

First marriages

Divorces

Remarriages

1961 1966 1971 1976 1981 1986 1991 1997

Chart 3
Women separated within five years of first marriage: by year of, and age at marriage, 1998–99

Percentages

	Age at marriage		
	Under 20	20–24	25–29
Year of marriage			
1965–1969	11	6	3
1970–1974	13	9	7
1975–1979	18	10	14
1980–1984	14	13	16
1985–1989	24	16	8

Chart 4
Children in families of couples divorced: by age of child

England & Wales   Thousands

	1971	1981	1991	1998
Under 5	21	40	53	40
Aged 5–10	41	68	68	68
Aged 11–15	21	52	40	43
All aged under 16	82	159	161	150
All couples divorcing	74	146	159	145

Chart 5
Families headed by lone parents as a percentage[1] of all families with dependent children: by marital status

Percentages

	1971	1976	1981	1986	1991–92	1996–97	1998–99
Lone mother							
Single	1	2	2	3	6	7	9
Widowed	2	2	2	1	1	1	1
Divorced	2	3	4	6	6	6	8
Separated	2	2	2	3	4	5	5
All lone mothers	7	9	11	13	18	20	22
Lone father	1	2	2	1	1	2	2
Married/cohabiting couple	92	89	87	86	81	79	75
All families with dependent children	100	100	100	100	100	100	100

[1] Dependent children are persons under 16, or aged 16 to 18 and in full-time education, in the family unit, and living in the household.

Chart 6
Births outside marriage as a percentage of all live births

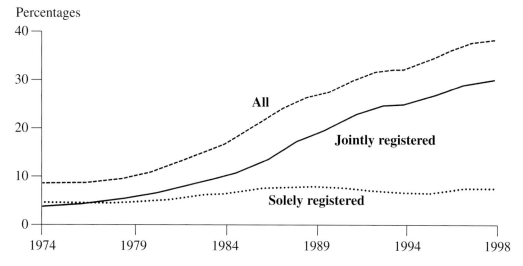

Percentages

All

Jointly registered

Solely registered

1974   1979   1984   1989   1994   1998

Chart 7
Fertility rates: by age of mother at childbirth

Live births per 1,000 women

	1961	1971	1981	1991	1997	1998
Under 20	37	50	28	33	30	31
20–24	173	154	107	89	75	74
25–29	178	155	130	120	105	102
30–34	106	79	70	87	89	90
35–39	51	34	22	32	39	40
40 and over	16	9	5	5	7	8
All ages	91	84	62	64	60	59

Chart 8
Percentage of women childless at age 25, 35 and 45[1]: by year of birth

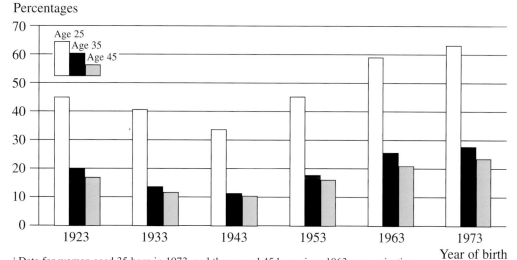

Percentages

Age 25
Age 35
Age 45

1923   1933   1943   1953   1963   1973
Year of birth

[1] Data for women aged 35 born in 1973, and those aged 45 born since 1963, are projections.
All other percentages are based on actual data up to the end of 1998.

Source: *Social Trends 30*
Office for National Statistics

Summarise the main conclusions about changes in the family, which can be drawn from these charts.

[9 marks]

BILL'S ANSWER

Chart 1 shows very clearly a number of the main trends relating to changes in the family. It shows steady increases in the number of single person households (people living on their own), lone parents with dependent children and in couples without children. The lone parents with dependent children are predominantly mothers, as is shown in Chart 5, which also shows a decline in the number of married or cohabiting couples.

Chart 2 supports this with the decline since the late 1960s in the number of marriages, coupled with an increase in the number of divorces. Chart 3 also supports this with increases in the number of women separated within five years of their first marriage, the highest figure being for women under 20. Chart 3 shows that nearly a quarter of the women who married between 1985 and 1989, under the age of 20 are now divorced. Chart 4 also shows how many more children are now living in families of couples divorced.

Chart 6 shows a steady increase in the number of children born outside marriage from just under 10% in 1974 to nearly 40% in 1998 and finally Charts 7 and 8 show fewer women are having children now than in 1961.

This direct approach is a very effective start and suggests confident command of the data. It would be safer to refer to **proportions** rather than numbers however.

This links up well and makes further points. There is one small slip – the reference to Chart 3 in the 3rd sentence should continue to say **'separated'** rather than 'divorced'

This final part is a little **short on detail** for Charts 7 and 8 although the single claim is correct. It lacks an **overall summary** statement.

How to score full marks

 Bill's answer is an effective one, which shows good command of key points in each of the charts. In terms of **approach and structure** it is a **model response**, well worth copying for this type of question. It is **systematic** in covering each of the charts and **direct** in picking out key features without wasting any words. Although in most cases it is correct to say that numbers of single persons, lone parents, etc are increasing, many of the charts are based on percentages, so it would be safer to refer to **percentages or proportions** as raw numbers can differ from these.

 One or two **further trends** in the charts are worth mentioning as key points:

- The increases in one-person households in Chart 1 relate both to younger and **older persons.**
- In Chart 2, just as the number of divorces has increased, so has the number of **remarriages.**
- As the number of first marriages has declined, the number of **divorces** (and children in divorced families) has **begun to 'tail off'** (Charts 2, 3 and 4), although if parents never marry (Charts 5 and 6) the number of separations may not show up and the **true family picture may be obscured** by this.
- A further feature of Charts 7 and 8 is that many women are **having children later** rather than not at all.

 Bill's answer could do with a **summary statement** to round it off, such as:

Altogether the charts show a decline in the conventional two-parent family and the number of children, as more people opt to live on their own or not to get married. Nevertheless for the majority, marriage or couples cohabiting remains the dominant pattern.

Don't forget ...

Look for some **significant feature or trend** in each set of data.

Think of **reasons** for any changes or differences.

Consider what each reason may contribute to an **overall picture.**

Try to decide what this contribution is and summarise it in as **few words** as possible.

Show the purpose of your answer in appropriate **opening and closing statements.**

Adjust the **number of points** you make and the amount of time you spend on your answer according to the **number of marks** available.

Source 6: WORLD ENERGY PRODUCTION AND CONSUMPTION

Chart 1: World's Top 10 Energy Producers and Consumers 1998

Million tonnes of oil equivalent

Producers		Consumers		Population (m)
USA	1835	USA	2389	274
Russian Federation	1034	China	855	1263
China	835	Russian Federation	655	147
Saudi Arabia	529	Japan	536	126
Canada	433	Germany	349	82
UK	293	India	315	998
India	251	Canada	299	31
Iran	249	France	252	61
Mexico	234	UK	246	59
Australia	209	Brazil	204	168
World total	**9631**	**World total**	**9519**	**5901**

Chart 2: Oil Imports and Exports 1999

Movements within regions indicated are not included (million tonnes)

	Crude exports	Crude imports	Balance of trade
USA	6.6	427.6	−421.0
Canada	58.4	40.6	17.8
Mexico	81.2	-	81.2
South & Central America	110.2	54.3	55.9
Western Europe	60.5	393.5	−333.0
Former Soviet Union	135.8	-	135.8
Central Europe	0.1	48.6	−48.5
Middle East	794.1	4.2	789.9
North Africa	99.3	7.7	91.6
West Africa	145.1	3.8	141.6
Eastern & Southern Africa	2.2	23.6	−21.4
Australasia	10.4	28.6	−18.2
China	7.9	36.6	−28.7
Japan	0.2	214.9	−214.7
Other Asia-Pacific	53.6	294.1	−240.5
Other	12.2	-	12.2
Total World	**1578.1**	**1578.1**	**0.0**

WORLD ENERGY RESERVES AND RATES OF CONSUMPTION

Chart 3: Proven Energy Reserves 1999

Oil (1000 million barrels)   Natural Gas (1 trillion cubic metres)   Coal (1 million tonnes)

	Oil	%	Gas	%	Coal	%
North America[1]	8.4	6.0	7.31	5.0	256 477	26.1
South & Central America	12.9	9.2	6.31	4.3	21 574	2.2
Europe	2.7	1.9	5.15	3.5	122 032	12.4
Former Soviet Union	9.0	6.4	56.70	38.7	230 178	23.4
Middle East	91.5	65.2	49.52	33.8	193	-
Africa	10.0	7.1	11.16	7.7	61 412	6.2
Asia-Pacific	5.9	4.2	10.28	7.0	292 345	29.7
World	**140.4**	**100**	**146.43**	**100**	**984 211**	**100**

[1] Canada, USA and Mexico

As a result of the uneven geography of production and consumption, energy sources are the largest single item in international trade. Taking the major example of oil, some regions are net exporters; others rely heavily on imported oil and so have to generate wealth by other means to be able to pay for their imports.

Proven energy reserves are also unevenly distributed. Reserves in the USA and the Russian Federation have declined and Europe's reserves are expected to dry up early this century. Central America and Africa are expected to cease oil exports around 2025.

Between 1989 and 1999 the world level of primary energy consumption increased by 11 per cent. This change was led by the Middle East with a 52 per cent increase, followed by South and Central America with a 38 per cent rise. Relatively costly energy in Europe depressed consumption to the comparatively low growth rate of 2 per cent, while the dissolution of the Soviet Union led to the collapse in consumption there by over a third. If rates of energy consumption were to remain constant, then it has been estimated that proven oil reserves would last forty years, natural gas sixty years and coal three hundred years. However, because consumption rates are increasing these estimates may need revision in the future.

ALTERNATIVE ENERGY SOURCES

Alternatives to traditional energy sources are nuclear power and renewable resources. Consumption of nuclear power has been at relatively low levels and has grown more slowly than traditional energy sources. Asia-Pacific and South and Central America have experienced the highest growth in the past decade, led by Japan, which generates two thirds of its electricity from nuclear sources. The question of sustainability has underpinned the search for new sources of energy which are less detrimental to the environment than traditional sources and nuclear power.

One proposed solution is conservation through increased energy efficiency, i.e. increasing the ratio of useful energy input to output. Other solutions lie in energy resources which are renewable, such as geothermal, wind, solar, biomass and hydropower. Around 5 per cent of total primary energy requirements in Australia, Austria, Canada, Denmark, Sweden and Switzerland are currently met by renewable energy. The most successful form of renewable energy to date has been hydroelectric power, consumption of which has risen over 20 per cent in world terms between 1989 and 1999 with South and Central America showing the largest rise (52 per cent), followed by Asia-Pacific (31 per cent).

Adapted from: *The Times Concise Atlas of the World* **2000**

Question types 3, 5 and 6

What do you consider to be the key features and implications of the data and information in this extract?

[9 marks]

Examiner's hints
- Use a similar approach to analysing the data and presenting your response as Bill does in the previous question on changes in the family.
- Write your answer in continuous prose and remember to comment on **both** the key features **and** implications of the data **and** information as you see them.

Answers can be found on pages 93–94.

Analysing knowledge and arguments is a requirement for all General Studies examinations, but this is tested slightly differently in the specifications. The questions in this chapter are specific to Edexcel Units 4 and 5 because of the distinctive style of questions they set to test this objective.

The other boards' questions are broader and more like those in the next chapter, but it is still worthwhile looking at this chapter and attempting the Question to Try. The detailed advice and information on categorising different types of knowledge and argument will be useful in answering questions from the other boards.

QUESTION AND STUDENT'S ANSWER

Source 7: TWO VIEWS OF MULTICULTURALISM IN BRITAIN

Mr Gerald Howarth (Conservative, Aldershot) speaking in the House of Commons 29th March 1999:

> Some unpalatable truths have to be faced, one of which is the fact that no Government has ever received a mandate to turn the United Kingdom into a multiracial society. Despite the warnings given in the 1960s and 1970s about the inevitable social consequences of large-scale immigration to Britain, successive Governments have ploughed on regardless.
>
> There are those who will use the report[1] to try to advance a cause that I do not believe to be in the interests of good race relations in this country. Some people who have come here freely and others who have sought refuge in this country appear no longer content to learn and accept our native customs and traditions, but wish to assert their own. Some of the minority even want to dictate to the majority.
>
> I believe that the report makes chilling reading in places …; there is the 'Orwellian' threat as it was described by David Maclean, MP – of indoctrination in our schools to make children 'value cultural diversity'. Although some people welcome cultural diversity, others see it as a threat and there is no point in this House being other than aware of that fact. It strikes some people that the homogeneity of the United Kingdom is somehow under threat.
>
> This country is Britain, and so the best service that we can do for all our children is to give them a thorough knowledge of the history and cultural heritage of these islands; Britain is a tolerant country and we need to keep working at good race relations, but it is time that those with ethnic minority backgrounds, just 6 per cent of the population, tried to be more understanding of us and our centuries-old culture.

[1]*Macpherson Report into the killing of Stephen Lawrence*

Mr David Lammy (Labour, Tottenham) making his first speech as the youngest MP in the UK, speaking in the House of Commons, 20th July 2000:

I stand here with great humility as the newly elected representative of the people of Tottenham. Hon. Members know that I stand here only because of the sad and sudden death of Bernie Grant. I would dearly have loved to spend my first years in Parliament working alongside Bernie. Fate determined that was not to be …

Although Tottenham is a constituency of much poverty, it has never been impoverished in its people. Through the centuries, many cultures of the world have traversed Tottenham High Road – white English people, Russians, Huguenots, Spaniards, Greek and Turkish Cypriots, Africans, Irish, Hasidic Jews, Asians, Caribbean islanders and, more recently, Kosovans and other people from eastern Europe. There is no need to go to New York or California to experience dynamic diversity and vibrancy. One need not look only to the Commonwealth for a model of communities coming together. Under our own eyes, people from the far reaches of the world are living happily together, from different backgrounds, races and religions.

All contribute to the richness of Tottenham. All understand the importance of unity and working and living together. All celebrate and glory in the multi-faith, multicultural family that constitutes Tottenham. These people are a valuable resource. If that resource was an untapped oilfield or a new diamond mine, business would be queuing round the block to buy the rights. People are the best and most precious resource that we have. I am acutely aware that I am here today because, at every stage of my development, people have invested in me.

I have had the support of a dedicated mother and family, Haringey council, Haringey teachers, my church, my secondary school, the Labour party, mentors in the legal profession and lecturers at the University of London and Harvard Law School … No one said, 'This isn't for you. Who do you think you are? Black men from Tottenham don't go to Harvard Law School.' People believed in me. They invested in me. Constituents such as mine want and deserve that same investment – investment in people and the funds and resources not just to take up employment, but to become self-employed by opening small businesses, dot.com enterprises, cafes and newsagents. They want to play football at White Hart Lane, play music in a band or create art. We must invest in people's souls as well as their skills.

(a) Which of the following statements from the text contain objective knowledge?

  (i) ... there is the 'Orwellian' threat – as it was described by David Maclean, MP – of indoctrination in our schools to make children 'value cultural diversity'. (Passage 1, paragraph 3)

  (ii) This country is Britain, and so the best service that we can do for all our children is to give them a thorough knowledge of the history and cultural heritage of these islands ... (Passage 1, paragraph 4)

  (iii) ... those with ethnic minority backgrounds, just 6 per cent of the population, ... (Passage 1, paragraph 4)

  (iv) Through the centuries, many cultures of the world have traversed Tottenham High Road – white English people, Russians, Huguenots, Spaniards, Greek and Turkish Cypriots, Africans, Irish, Hasidic Jews, Asians, Caribbean islanders and, more recently, Kosovans and other people from eastern Europe. (Passage 2, paragraph 2)

    A Statement **(i)**
    B Statements **(i)** and **(ii)**
    C Statements **(ii)** and **(iii)**
    D Statements **(iii)** and **(iv)**
    E None of these statements   [1 mark]

(b) What type of knowledge is contained in the following statement?
Under our own eyes, people from the far reaches of the world are living happily together, from different backgrounds, races and religions. (Passage 2, paragraph 2)

    A Scientific knowledge
    B Objective knowledge
    C Subjective knowledge
    D Knowledge based on moral values
    E None of these   [1 mark]

(c) Select **two** short extracts from any part(s) of either passage and state the type(s) of argument they contain.   [2 marks]

(d) In which passage is the argument justified more successfully?
Support your answer with reasons related to the types of knowledge and argument used.   [8 marks]

[Additional marks for quality of written communication 3 marks]

[**Total 15 marks**]

LEILA'S ANSWER

(a) C Statements (ii) and (iii)   0/1

(b) C Subjective knowledge   1/1

How to score full marks

 Statement **(iii)** is **objective** knowledge because it is based on a **verifiable fact** (… just 6% of the population) Statement **(ii)**, although it starts with a factual statement (This country is Britain …), is really making a claim about 'the **best** service that we can do for all our children', and this is a **subjective** statement. The other statement which is essentially factual and therefore can be called objective is **(iv)** (… many cultures of the world have traversed Tottenham High Road …). Therefore **D** is the correct answer to **(a)**. **Note** also that it is not necessary with multiple choice (objective test) questions to indicate anything more than the letter you think represents the correct answer.

LEILA'S ANSWER

(c) (1) Britain is a tolerant country (line 14) is an example of a subjective argument, because it is based on the authors (Mr Gerald Howarth) own view.

   (2) 'We must invest in people's souls as well as their skills' at the end of the second article is a good example of an inductive argument because in this paragraph the author (Mr David Lammy) argues that when you believe and invest in people they will succeed like he has.   1/2

How to score full marks

 (2) is a correct answer as the question is testing your knowledge about **types of argument**. In (1) 'Britain is a tolerant country' is **not a type** of argument in this context, it is simply a statement – the author's belief – that is indeed subjective, but not what the question is seeking here.

LEILA'S ANSWER

(d) I think that the arguments are justified more successfully in the second passage as Mr David Lammy is a black man and therefore has a better knowledge of what he is talking about than Mr Howarth who seems quite prejudice_ and just a little bit racist in his remarks.

Although both passages contain quite good arguments to support their case, Mr Lammy is talking from personal experience and this makes his arguments stronger. Also Mr Howarth is virtually saying that all minorities should behave in a more British way, whereas Mr Lammy is promoting the cause of cultural diversity, which I think makes much more sense. You cannot just turn foreigners into true, blue English people overnight and this is what Mr Howarth seems to expect.

However, both speeches are quite emotional and although both try to make use of facts and arguments to prove their case, both seem to be based on the belief that society should behave more in one way rather than another (i.e. more multicultural or not) and try to persuade the listener that their way is right. In the end it all depends upon what you believe in — should minority groups have to change their customs to fit our way or should we change ours to fit theirs? It is up to the individual to decide.

4/8

Quality of written communication: 3/3   Total 9/15

How to score full marks

 Some of the points Leila makes in (d) meet the requirements of the question and gain marks, but many are just too personal and subjective; they relate to whether she agrees with the case being made, rather than analysing the type of knowledge and arguments being used. Her answer needs to be **more analytical** and justify more clearly the claims she is making. For example, both claims in the first paragraph need **more explanation**; otherwise they are just her personal opinion.

 The first sentence of the second paragraph provides some justification, but Leila should have gone on to **explain why** she thinks both passages contain 'quite good (= justified?) arguments'. She could have said that the first speaker draws on historical knowledge ('no Government has ever received a mandate …'), or the opinions of others (David Maclean), or straightforward facts ('just 6 per cent of the population') to support his arguments.

Leila's commentary in the second part of the second paragraph is fair enough, but it is just a summary of the cases being made rather than an **analysis of how they are made**. She partly justifies her own point of view, but this is not what the question is seeking.

The first part of the third paragraph is more in line with what is required and quite perceptive. Again it would have been even better if Leila had gone on to **illustrate and explain** how the speakers had used 'facts and arguments to support their case' (what facts? what arguments?). She could have said that Mr Lammy draws on his personal knowledge of the existing multicultural mix in Tottenham to make the case for the benefits of cultural diversity, which he likens to 'an untapped oilfield or a new diamond mine' (argument by analogy).

The final point would **not** receive any marks because, although it may be valid in its own right, it is more to do with what Leila thinks about the topic and is outside the question, like some of her earlier comments.

There are 3 marks available for quality of written communication and Leila gets full marks because she:
- uses a **form** and **style of writing** appropriate to **purpose** and **subject matter** (1 mark)
- organises relevant material **clearly** and **coherently**, using **specialist vocabulary** where appropriate (1 mark)
- writes **legibly** with **accurate use of spelling**, **grammar** and **punctuation** in order to make meaning clear. Although she has made two mistakes in omitting the apostrophe from author's in (c)(1) and d from prejudiced in (d), the meaning is perfectly clear (1 mark).

Key points to remember

- This type of question is testing your knowledge and understanding of Assessment Objective 4 (AO4) in a very specific way **particular to Edexcel** papers. You must know the difference between **types of 'knowledge' and 'argument'**. It is vital not to confuse these and the questions need to be answered very precisely. Therefore you need to understand and be able to apply the following rigorously:

Types of knowledge	Example
Scientific	based on observation and experiment, e.g. The Moon revolves around the Earth, and the Earth revolves around the Sun.
Objective	based on facts which can be verified and agreed, regardless of feelings, e.g. Picasso painted the picture called *Guernica*.
Subjective	based on opinions or beliefs, e.g. Britain is a more racially tolerant society than it used to be.
Based on belief	accepted as true or the 'best' explanation (but cannot be fully proven and not everybody would agree), e.g. Jane is clever (because her teacher says so) or Building more roads aids economic growth.
Based on moral values	accepted as right or wrong, e.g. Pornography is bad because it demeans human beings or Large companies which make huge profits are cheating people.

Types of argument	Example
Deductive	argues from the general to the particular, i.e. it follows automatically, e.g. if the angles of a triangle = 180°, and in a particular triangle 2 angles sum to 120°, then the third angle must = 60°. If the premiss is true, the conclusion is also true. Many mathematical models are of this type.
Inductive	argues from the particular to the general, i.e. a series of events or experiences point to something being true, e.g. water (usually) boils at 100°C. Science is inductive in the sense that studying evidence empirically (i.e. testing to see if something exists or happens) leads to the formation of a law or theory, which allows you to predict what is there or will happen when the same situation is repeated. David Lammy uses an inductive argument in the passage when he says that when you believe and invest in people, they will thrive. It is not as certain as a scientific law, but it can count as a sociological or psychological theory, perhaps.
From cause	arises when one circumstance invariably correlates with another, the two are causally related, e.g. every time a person eats more calories than they expend, that person gains weight. No person gains weight without eating more calories than they expend. Therefore, when a person eats more calories than they expend, this causes them to gain weight.
From analogy	uses an illustration or comparison which appears similar and applies it to a different case, e.g. as David Lammy does in his reference to people from different cultures being like 'an untapped oilfield or a new diamond mine'. The weakness of such arguments is that for an argument from analogy to hold good, the two cases must have identical features. Any differences would undermine it.
From authority	is claiming that something is true because some knowledgeable person or expert source says that it is, e.g. stealing is wrong because it is written in the Bible, or genetically modified food has not been shown to be harmful because the Government's chief scientist has said so. Such arguments only hold good up to the point where you can believe wholly in the source being right.
To the person	is similar to arguing from authority, except that the case is usually based on the integrity of the person making the argument, i.e. something is true (or not true) because the person referred to would never (always) lie. Such arguments are false, because it is the evidence for the argument itself that should decide.
From lack of evidence	is seeking to claim that something is true because there is no evidence to prove it is not. This is false because there must be evidence either way to decide whether something is true or false.

Source 8: WHAT SHOULD WE DO WITH YOUR GENES?

This week's publication of a detailed codebook of human genes is undoubtedly a scientific milestone, but will it affect your life? Have you been left with the expectation that an end to all inherited human diseases is just around the corner? Or maybe you have been haunted by the spectre of a world in which genetic flaws are ruthlessly weeded out to create a race of superhumans?

Whatever the impact, one thing is certain: you cannot leave the scientists to just get on and decide how knowledge of the human genome should be used to shape our future. The time has come for all of us to engage in the debate about how best to use the products of this scientific achievement.

It is difficult to overstate how dramatically an understanding of this blueprint for life will affect the quality of our existence. Medicine has started to tackle some inherited human diseases, but there is now the real prospect that we will discover how genes control or influence all illnesses.

But such a bright future cannot be realised without tackling some major social and ethical, as well as scientific, problems. For instance, how do we decide which diseases to tackle first? At present, our understanding of individual genetic disorders is based mainly on identifying a defect in a single gene, which, when present, always results in a disease, as with Gaucher's, Huntington's, cystic fibrosis or sickle cell anaemia. There are thousands of such illnesses, many of them severe, but they only affect very small proportions of the population.

However, studies of the genome are now revealing how our chances of suffering from more common illness, such as diabetes, Alzheimer's, heart disease and asthma, also depend on our DNA. This link has been difficult to see before because it is a number of variations in many different genes that control our susceptibility.

As scientists begin the long process of finding out the functions of each of the 30,000 or so human genes, it seems likely that we will be able to develop predictive diagnostic tests and then to produce preventative medicines that can reduce the odds of falling victim to any single illness.

In an ideal world, we could investigate each of these diseases simultaneously. But with a finite supply of both scientists and funding, we have to prioritise our research efforts. To what extent should public dialogue play a role in deciding which illnesses researchers should concentrate on initially? And whose suffering should be tackled first?

The development of new treatments and medicines will cost money, of course, and its products, in the form of medicines and therapies, may be expensive and in short supply, to begin with anyway. Most people in this country are uncomfortable with the notion that access to good health should depend on your ability to afford it. Would you be happy to see the benefits of this made available only to a wealthy few?

Of course, finding out that you are genetically more likely to develop an illness can be a troubling psychological burden, particularly if a treatment or cure is not yet available. Few people would relish being presented with a list of genetically related diseases together with the individually calculated probabilities that you will fall victim to them. Balanced against this is the cost to everybody else if you are willingly ignorant of the potential threats.

Still more contentious is the question of who else should know about your likelihood of developing certain afflictions. Should insurance companies be allowed to adjust premiums if they find out that you are more likely to succumb to a fatal disease? Should potential employers take into account that you have a higher than average chance of falling prey to a debilitating condition? These are questions about how far the science of genomics should impinge on our daily lives. Scientists can tell us what is possible, but society needs some consensus about how far genomics should influence our existence.

In addition, there is the consideration of how we fund these advances. Are we willing to pay higher taxes, or see a redistribution of current funding, to allow faster progress in research and realise the maximum benefits in the shortest time possible?

In the long run, healthcare based on genomics is likely to save us money. At present, most of medicine is focused on the relatively expensive business of treating the symptoms of an illness. With an understanding of genetic susceptibility to these diseases, more effort can be directed towards prevention, by controlling the environmental factors that might trigger illness or, indeed, correcting or compensating for the genetic flaw that causes the risk.

It is not difficult to see how money and human misery might be saved – if, for instance, a DNA flaw preventing insulin production in the pancreas could be corrected to prevent diabetes appearing, rather than coping with daily insulin shots. But how much of the groundwork research are we prepared to fund to achieve this advancement?

Perhaps even more ethically challenging is the question of how far we should be allowed to interfere with the genetic make-up of our children. It is illegal in the UK to alter the genetic make-up of sperm and eggs, but will society one day decide it is permissible to correct genetic defects before fertilising to avoid passing on a potentially dangerous condition?

The science of genomics has a great deal to offer society, and should spark a revolution in medicine and healthcare. The magnitude of the changes that we may experience in our daily lives as a result make it imperative that scientists, policy-makers and the public listen to each other. Recent experiences with GM crops and BSE have shown the unhappy consequences of a breakdown in this communication.

It is vital that the dialogue about how we apply our knowledge of the human genome is successful so that we can seize this wonderful opportunity to improve our own lives and those of future generations.

Source: Adapted from Michael Dexter & Robert May,
The Daily Telegraph 14 February 2001

Question types 4 and 6

(a) Identify **two** objective and **two** subjective assertions in Dexter and May's article.

[4 marks]

(b) Explain why Dexter and May's article could be considered to be an unjustified argument.

[8 marks]

[Additional marks for quality of written communication 3 marks]

[Total 15 marks]

Examiner's hints
- Make sure you know exactly what an 'assertion' is before answering **(a)**.
- Note that **(b)** requires you to explain why the article could be considered to be **unjustified** argument, i.e. evaluate the arguments and demonstrate why they may not be justified. You are not asked to give your own opinion or say why you agree or disagree with the views expressed. You should restrict your comments to the nature and quality of the **authors'** arguments.

Answers can be found on pages 94–95.

5 ANALYSING KNOWLEDGE AND ARGUMENTS, ASSESSING VALIDITY AND VALUE OF A SOURCE

The questions in this chapter are broader than those in the previous chapter, but they are designed to assess similar objectives. They are about evaluating the knowledge and arguments used in the sources and the validity and value of the case presented. Above all, the questions require you to consider the sources **objectively**, regardless of your own opinions: to analyse what sort of knowledge and arguments are being used. How sound and supported are they? What are the strengths and weaknesses of the case being made?

QUESTION AND STUDENT'S ANSWER

Source 9: 'MY CAR IS A NECESSITY. IT'S NOT A LUXURY.'

*That's the feeling of British Motorists surveyed by the AA for its **Living With The Car** report. The AA asked thousands of members what they felt about life with their cars – and other people's. John Dawson reports on what you say are your top concerns and why there will be two million more car owners by the year 2000.*

Taken as a 'snapshot', the AA *Living With The Car* survey shows members enjoying lives built around the car. Decisions about where to live and work, to shop and socialise, depend on it. And the arrival of children only intensities the dependency: as one busy mum reflected, 'my middle name is chauffeur'.

In fact, a staggering 96 per cent of drivers told the AA that being able to drive is either essential or important. Over half said getting to work would be difficult without the car and nearly 70 per cent said the same about leisure trips. Love it or hate it, most homes have a car and are prepared to give up much else for the opportunities it brings. Most people run the best car they can afford and spend a remarkably fixed proportion of their income – around 15 per cent – on it. The more we earn, the better the car we run. Motoring is no longer the preserve of the well-to-do; seven out of 10 homes now have at least one car. Car ownership is lowest in the urban centres where walking, cycling and public transport are all workable alternatives. In the country, by contrast, where a car is usually essential, even homes on very low incomes tend to run one.

Wherever we live, it's clear there are more vehicles on the road, particularly on trunk routes. Car traffic is growing partly because we're travelling further. One member commented that, 'I work for about seven different companies. I have to travel from one to another.' Another said, 'You can travel 30 miles to your job now.' With most couples now fielding two earners, one partner will often travel further to a better job rather than uproot the family – especially when the new job might not last that long. When a family purchases its first or second car, it's often because someone needs it to get to work at a place or time which public transport can't easily serve. Politicians boast of Britain's 'flexible labour market' – flexibility, it seems, also built around the car.

Britain has 29 million drivers but only 12 million are women. This is changing fast because just as many women are now obtaining driving licences. The car is becoming central to the lives of an increasing number of women, bringing them access to the kind of employment and social activities that men take for granted. But equality has not arrived just yet. In a family, the woman's car is far more likely to be sold if rising motoring costs mean that one car has to go: two-thirds of homes with two cars reported this was the case. Women travel two-thirds of the mileage of men but make more trips as they juggle the demands of home and work to tight personal schedules. One female member said of her car. 'It's my lifeline … I wouldn't be able to go out as often as I do. Now I can just get in and go.' Over 80 per cent of women would rather not use buses, trains or the London Underground alone at night. Women feel safest in their cars. 'I would hate to be wandering around some of these places and not have the safety of a car around me,' said one member. That said, many more women than men are concerned about driving alone at night.

Britons are living and driving longer so there is a growing number of older drivers. Many older people have been driving all their adult life and are increasingly dependent on their cars. One such driver responded to the survey by saying, 'If I didn't have the car, the kids would have to come to me all the time; that would make me feel very lonely.' Today, more than half those over 65 have a driving licence. In 20 years' time it will be more than four in five and more than half will be women. The AA is working with the medical professions, car manufacturers and highway engineers to ensure that we prepare for this future. The survey highlights the importance of encouraging both partners to share the driving. One recently widowed member said: 'Suddenly you're on your own. You think, I can't do it. I've got to do it!'

Young drivers make up another rapidly growing group of motorists. Most teenagers intend to learn to drive and their 17th birthday is more important to them than ever. For some parents that can't be a day too soon: as one young driver said, 'My mum used to joke about her being a taxi cab.' Major efforts have been made by the AA to make sure young people learn to drive safely. The AA's driving school, for example, is the only major school that insists on fully qualified instructors. And the new Driver's Act, which came into force in June 1997, was researched and proposed by the AA. The minority of new drivers who run up motoring offences like cricket runs will now have to resit their tests if they continue to be irresponsible.

About 10 per cent of Britain's population has a disability that makes using ordinary public transport difficult or impossible. The first choice of disabled people is their own car. Ninety-five per cent of disabled motorists say that driving their own car allows them to be more independent. If they have a car, they make 40 per cent more trips each week than if they don't. One disabled driver commented: 'Sadly, we get out very little because we don't have a vehicle … we have no means of going anywhere together.'

[An AA/National Opinion Poll survey of drivers' top six transport concerns in 1996 showed motoring cost issues and road safety as the top concerns of 73% of drivers with environmental pollution coming sixth.]

Source: *AA Members Magazine* Autumn 1997

Question types 4, 6 and 7

Discuss the strengths and weaknesses of this source as a contribution to the debate
about transport problems. [9 marks]

Harriet is right to start by
commenting on the origin of
the source, but the AA is better
described as an organisation
whose major purpose is to
represent the interests of
motorists.

Other weaknesses in Harriet's
argument:

● the fact that the article was
written in 1997 does not
necessarily make it out of date

● the survey is only
representative of the AA's
own members.

The first sentence is valid, but
the remainder of the
paragraph is just descriptive
and needs to be better linked
to the question.

This strays from the point. The
question asks for comments
about the weakness of the
article whereas this is more
about the weakness of the car
as a means of transport and
the discussion about congestion
charges has become irrelevant.

This first sentence more or less
repeats the point made at the
beginning of the second
paragraph, and again the
remainder of the discussion is
not focusing on the point of the
question.

HARRIET'S ANSWER

This article is from the AA Members Magazine Autumn
1997, which is quite a long time ago, so it is out of date
and many things have changed since then. Therefore the
information it gives is not very reliable. The AA is also an
organisation which provides motor insurance and so you would
expect it to be on the side of the car and drivers as
the more cars there are, the more money they will earn
and so it could be rather biased. One good thing though is
that the survey asked thousands of members, which means
it is quite representative.

A strength of the article is that it shows how much
people need their cars and that they are prepared to
make sacrifices to own one. People who need their cars
most are those who live in the country because there is
little or no public transport and they need them to get to
work and to do the weekly shopping. Women also need
cars because they do not feel safe on public transport,
particularly at night, and many disabled people would not be
able to get out all if they did not have a car.

A weakness though is that there are too many cars on
the road, and how much pollution and congestion they cause.
I am in favour of congestion charging which Ken Livingstone
has introduced in London. I think it should be introduced in
other major cities such as Manchester and Liverpool where
the rush-hour traffic is horrendous and the average speed
can be as little as 11 mph. They should also gradually
introduce charges for motorways as driving on the M6 is
impossible these days and something has to be done to
reduce the amount of cars using this road.

I think the article is a good article because it shows how
important the car is to almost everybody and the
government needs to know this when they make their
plans for transport, but I do think that people should be
encouraged to use public transport more, or where possible
to walk or use a bike, instead of just hopping into the
car when they feel like it. It's too easy and what
are we going to do when all the oil runs out? (3/9)

How to score full marks

 This is a weak response with few of the points scoring marks. Harriet needs to **focus more precisely on the question** – the strengths and weaknesses **of the source** – and less on what she thinks of the issues. What makes the arguments used in the article strong and what makes them weak?

 Strengths

- draws directly on a **substantial** survey (thousands of members) and represents motorists' opinions and experience in an **authoritative** way
- 70% of the households own at least one car and this is **evidence** of how widespread the issues and concerns are
- argues the case for the car and the interests of motorists **persuasively** within the wider transport debate
- **illustrates** why cars are needed and the inadequacy of public transport in a range of circumstances (for those living in the country, needing to get to work, travelling late at night, disabled)
- **demonstrates** how the number of drivers (women, young people and older people) will increase and that resulting problems will need to be addressed.

 Weaknesses

- uses **partial and biased** arguments; is only concerned about the car and the interests of motorists and deliberately **ignores alternatives**
- has a **direct financial interest** in increasing membership and promoting the use of the car (rescue service, insurance, purchase loans)
- **not wholly representative** and speaking only for its own members; what about people who do not belong to the AA and the 30% of households which do not possess a car?
- uses a lot of **anecdotal evidence** from individuals to support its arguments
- inclined to **self-advertisement**; what the AA is doing itself to address some of the problems (own driving school).

Don't forget ...

This type of question is testing **similar** skills to the questions on Sources 7 and 8 (pages 25–33) but in a **broader** way. It is seeking **overall evaluation** of the article in a wider debate.

The source is part of a larger Case Study of several documents on transport issues in the UK and further extracts from this Case Study also appear as Sources 1 and 11. Candidates for **AQA Specification A** would have the opportunity to study these in advance. You would be expected to be aware of a **wide range of concerns and different arguments** on the issues and to have done some analysis of these **in advance**. This would include checking on the **origins of sources** and developing some opinions about their **credibility**. See page 7 for more general advice about how to prepare pre-release material.

Source 10: THE IMPACT OF CHANGES IN INFORMATION AND COMMUNICATIONS TECHNOLOGY

Petrarch had his quills. Trollope had his nibs. Journalists of old had their Remington typewriters clogged with ash and stained with coffee. Now we have computers. Mine is ten years old and must be replaced. As it creaks its last it has been declared obsolete, as has its language. I have arrived at the doors of the great god Windows and must learn its tricks. It is scarcely believable that ten years of software development has produced a system that is incomparably worse than its predecessor, a fact that even its salesmen blithely admit. Oh, said mine, technology does not always advance.

The impact of the word-processor on modern writing is a favourite topic among practitioners. We can correct, check and transmit words directly into newspapers. We can type as fast as we can think and print even faster. We are the cheetahs of the written word. No wonder modern novels are gigantic affairs. Modern newspapers are equally gargantuan, in part because computer-printing has sent costs plummeting. Words come cheap when they have Intel inside.

The word-processor changed everything. Like the mobile phone it was a true revolution. What had once taken sheafs of paper, a sub-editing desk, a library of cuttings and a hot-metal typesetting machine, was now in my lap. I could press a modem button and my work was sent to press. It was as near a perfect writing machine as technology could produce. Yet it is now obsolete and out of production.

The contrast with Windows is total, proof positive that scientific advance is sometimes a retard. The Windows system may suit business analysts and fashion designers. But for those who seek simple efficiency in their daily tools, it is to be avoided. My new machine takes longer to load, uses more power, has a shorter battery life and is heavier to carry. Using it is like wandering through a maze of maddening and useless alleys. Computer design had dumbed down with a vengeance.

Dr Johnson maintained that 'what is written without effort is in general read without pleasure'. The converse is that good writing comes hard. Looking back through my handwritten school essays I was surprised at how few crossings-out they contained. Today I would have re-written them five times over. I am sure the reason was that they were physically hard to write. The slowness of the hand disciplined the brain. The casual facility of the computer leads to sloppiness.

Equally the e-mail, unlike the handwritten letter, is emotionally ponderous. This electronic Eros is said to have revived the art of the lover's letter. Millions of these missives now flow down the lines where previously there was only idle chatter. Hurrah for that. At least e-mails are written in a sort of English and a sort of grammar. But the words printed on the screen pack a monotonous punch. Their meaning becomes distorted in transmission. Printed words written in haste lack the care and character of handwriting.

Yet this is surely a defunct cause. Handwriting is becoming a defunct skill. It is the Cinderella 'R'. Barely a month passes without a politician deploring the state of the 'three Rs'. Yet only two are ever cited, reading and arithmetic. Amid all this back to basics, there was no mention of writing. There was no curse on word-processors, no demand for a revival of glorious copperplate or slender italic.

In the artless age, handwriting was the nearest many children came to appreciating the beauty of shape, the flow of line and the pleasure of neatness. Since the earliest pictograms, writing has been an aesthetic exercise, as well as a means of communication.

To the monarchs of the British curriculum, the culture of primary education is now made up of reading and maths. As far as writing is concerned, pupils are expected to mark time. Any old scrawl will do as children wait their turn at the keyboard, to go 'on message'. Why bother to teach joined-up writing when IBM will do the job for you?

We need to curse a bit. But I am sure Bill Gates has the measure of us. Watch out for the next edition of Windows. This will be a back to basics program of even more fiendish complexity. Out will go the mouse and in will come the quill. We shall have to move it by hand laboriously over the lighted surface, stopping occasionally for ink. The printer will use parchment or vellum. And when the work is done, we shall take out from our sack a scrap of blotting paper, and dab our tears from the screen.

Source: Adapted from 'A Luddite's lament' by Simon Jenkins,
***The Times* 24 January 1998**

Question types 4, 6 and 7

Simon Jenkins tends to be critical of the impact of information technology on the education and communication skills of young people. To what extent, and for what reasons, do you agree or disagree with his judgment?

[50 marks]

Examiner's hints
- The focus of the question is Simon Jenkins' views on 'the impact of IT on the **education and communication skills of young people**' and not just whether you agree or disagree with his wider assessment of the new technology.
- Also important in the question are '**To what extent, and for what reasons . . .**'. The first gives you freedom to argue your own case and opinions, perhaps based on your own experiences, but you do not necessarily have to come down finally on one side or another. You may want to agree on some points but not on others.
- The question does **not require** you to formulate an overall judgement or final conclusion, although you may wish to, if you have a clear view on the benefits of IT in education and communication skills.
- Above all you should focus on the **nature and quality of the arguments**. What kind of knowledge and arguments are used? How sound and valid are they? How are they supported?

Answers can be found on page 95.

This chapter contains the broadest of the types of questions set on sources, but they are slightly more specific to the source and not quite as broad as the essays based on sources looked at in Section B, Chapter 4. The questions require you to be able to summarise in your own words the content of a source or sources, as well as evaluate them and respond to specific questions about them. This can mean giving your own opinions on the topic, if the question requires this, but as always these opinions must be supported and justified with reasons.

QUESTION AND STUDENT'S ANSWER

Source 11: CAR MAKERS STILL MILES AWAY FROM A CLEAN GREEN ALTERNATIVE

For Tony Appleton from Essex, the answer to the fuel shortage was sitting in the back of his garage: a Sinclair C5 electric car that had been unused for a decade, *writes Deborah Collcutt*. Like other attempts to overtake the internal combustion engine, the C5 was a brave failure. But it may be only a matter of time, and dwindling oil stocks, before a viable alternative to petrol and diesel has to be found.

This week, Sinclair said that he intended to bring out a new range of battery-powered vehicles. 'I am going to launch a new lightweight electric car and an electric scooter,' he said. 'I always knew a fuel crisis would come.' With even better commercial timing, Toyota launched a hybrid petrol/electric car, the Prius, on Friday. It already has a rival in a hybrid model from Honda, called the Insight. General Motors (GM) has plans for a fully functioning family saloon that has a small normal engine supplemented by batteries. And at this year's Birmingham motor show, Ford will be exhibiting an electric car called Th!nk.

In reality, however, electric cars will not be seen on a widespread basis for many years because they still cannot deliver high enough speeds and because the infrastructure needed for motorists to 'plug in' for recharging is costly.

Natural gas is another possibility. The supermarket chain Safeway already has seven distribution lorries that run on natural gas. But in the longer term, the same problems as with other fossil fuels apply.

Other, more complex technologies are being researched at vast expense, with fuel cells seen as one of the most promising. In a fuel cell system, an energy source such as natural gas or methanol is broken down to generate hydrogen, which is combined with oxygen to generate electricity. A fuel cell does not run down or require recharging in the same sense as a conventional battery. It will produce energy as long as fuel is supplied.

Without mass production, however, the system does not come cheap. The first production fuel cell cars – due on the roads by 2003/4 – are likely to cost substantially more than petrol or diesel vehicles. In the medium term, fuel cells and natural gas vehicles are likely to prove more suitable for commercial vehicle operators – particularly municipal bus operators or refuse collection services – than for private motorists. For fleet vehicles, the infrastructure obstacles can be overcome by establishing central fuelling depots, and could offset initial capital costs.

Despite the difficulties, even traditional car makers and oil companies acknowledge that the future of the internal combustion engine is limited. Ford has teamed up with BP Amoco to explore environmentally friendly road transport. GM has joined forces with Exxon on research into fuel cells.

For the moment, however, the problem is that, despite the European fuel protests, in the world's largest car market, petrol is still cheap and the incentives for pushing alternatives are limited. In America, a gallon of petrol still costs between £1.10 and £1.25 – less than a bottle of mineral water. Most industry analysts believe the real pressure to develop an alternative will have to come from tougher emissions controls in America. California has drawn up the country's stiffest emissions legislation and other states have introduced regulations dictating the use of alternative fuels in government vehicles.

But even before newer, cleaner engine technologies arrive, there may be other measures introduced with the aim of cutting petrol driven congestion and pollution in Britain. More effective than high levels of duty on petrol, say experts, are charges for those who use busy roads at peak times. 'Congestion charging could be a powerful tool for raising revenue and managing traffic demand,' said Professor David Begg, Head of the Government's Commission on Integrated Transport. 'Satellite technology that will allow congestion charging is already here, which eliminates the need to stop drivers at toll booths. If congestion charges were linked to reductions in fuel duty, suddenly a driver in the Highlands whose car trip has less environmental impact might be paying lower fuel charges, lower car tax and low congestion charges. As it is, some poorer rural Scottish households spend up to 60% of their travel budget on fuel.'

Source: *The Sunday Times* September 2000

Question types 8 and 9

Discuss to what extent new technologies offer a solution to the United Kingdom's transport problems. [9 marks]

HARRY'S ANSWER

New technologies offer fuel alternatives that do not pollute the atmosphere like petrol does. These new fuels for cars will eventually have to be used as oil, which is a fossil fuel, is running out. One idea is to use electricity. This would be clean and environmentally friendly. However, at the moment electrically run cars are too expensive.

Natural gas is another possibility and is already in use in some lorries, but this is not a renewable fuel and will also run out. Other more complex technologies are being researched using a lot of funding. Fuel cells are one option but will not be cheap enough until they are in mass production.

Almost anything can be used for fuel as long as it can be burned to release energy. Cars can theoretically be run on animal waste, sugar, alcohol, rape-seed oil and even rubbish. Gene technology could be used to manufacture a crop that has a very high, concentrated energy store and can be easily burned.

Satellite technology could be used for congestion charging which could relieve the worst traffic problems. This could be combined with reductions in fuel duty for more environmentally friendly cars, reducing the impact of transport on the environment. Road pricing could be used electronically to reduce traffic in congested areas. New smartcard technology means that police can track the electronic devices and a charge is automatically deducted when the driver crosses into the city centre.

Direct, to the point and gives a reason. More could be said about electric cars.

Another two explained points, but again there could be more development, particularly about fuel cells.

Good use of own knowledge which is permissible in the question, but also undeveloped and ignoring the 'to what extent . . .' aspect.

This is valid and summarises options given in the passage, but more development is needed on limitations throughout.

How to score full marks

 This is a competent response but it **is too focused on how** new technology could solve the problems rather than **the extent** to which it might solve them, taking into account limitations and issues. 'Discuss to what extent ...' requires **an evaluation of how effective** possible measures might be. A full discussion would include some of the following:

- electric car (heavy, slow and limited distance before re-charging required)
- hybrid petrol/electric car (slow, inadequate infrastructure to maintain it)
- natural gas (limited supply and fossil fuel source)
- fuel cell (expensive, more suitable for commercial vehicles)
- more efficient and 'cleaner' engines using current fuels (have to be replaced sooner or later)
- road charging (untried technology)
- are these likely to solve problem of congestion caused by too many vehicles?
- alternatives to the car need to be made more attractive to change people's habits and transport choices
- more effective solutions might be greater investment in public transport and other options (walking, cycling, car clubs).

Harry has managed to touch on most of these points taken from the mark scheme, as well as some of his own, but in each case **more evaluation is needed**. He almost certainly has not exploited his knowledge and ideas to the full and with a bit more care and concentration on the question he could easily have got closer to full marks. A useful **clue** for the **focus of an answer** to the question can be found in the **title of the article** 'Car makers still miles away ...'

Don't forget ...

This is another 'To what extent ...' question because many of the issues are entrenched social or ethical problems, and do not have simple answers. As we have said before, **you are not expected to solve them** at a stroke with a single solution. The fact that there are no single or ready answers is one of the reasons why the question has been asked.

You should normally try to take a **balanced and objective view** considering the **strengths and weaknesses** of the points you are proposing and **recognising their limitations**. Potentially you will gain more marks this way.

Source 12: OLD PEOPLE AND SOCIETY

Source A

Before our very eyes, politics is changing for older people. Policy-makers have finally awoken to the enormous importance of older voters, just as retailers now defer to the older shopper. When today's toddlers reach their prime, every third person in Britain will be over 60.

There is still the obstacle of ageism to contend with, and old age is associated with stigma, deprivation and loneliness, but there is also a new assertiveness among older people. More and more of them are declaring: 'I can say what I like and I can do what I like.'

After almost 40 years in journalism, half of it on *The Guardian*, I have spent much of the past 18 months editing a book of older people's views for the charity Help the Aged. I have found that they are not by any means sweet old things who ask for a seat on the bus; they are demanding a turn behind the driver's wheel.

Lady Margaret Simey – 'just plain Margaret, if you please' – is already a nonagenarian. I rang her one evening to discuss an unclear sentence and, once we had dealt with that, her voice suddenly changed. 'What on earth has happened to outrage?' she demanded. 'There is a hell of a lot in this life to be furious about – and not just things affecting older people – and yet everybody seems to be taking it all so easy. We want more outrage.'

Source B

Outside Buckingham Palace four months ago, two sixtysomething film stars exemplified polarised approaches to growing old. There was Dame Elizabeth Taylor – satiate yourself and live for today, lovers and all. Alongside her was Dame Julie Andrews – starved, monogamous, surviving for tomorrow without a single crow's foot. Soon, thanks to William the worm, the rest of us might be able to delay the choice between being Cleopatra and Sister Maria for another half century. William couldn't be less photogenic than his counterpart, Dolly the sheep. But news that 'SCS' drugs have helped prolong the negatode worm's life has been greeted by millions of humans who want to prolong their lives too.

The advances now being celebrated by scientists – whereby drugs mimic the body's own defences to illness – will transform medicine. Keen to see off the creationist tendency, some behind the Anglo-American research project have dismissed the idea that, if William's life span can be lengthened, so can ours. They are being disingenuous.

For if we have to 'reconsider ageing as an inevitability', as the researchers say, we also have to confront the possibility of living 30, 40 or 50 years longer. If worms can go on turning, and turning, and turning, so might we.

What the backers of the nematode worm project have happily acknowledged is that their findings could help prevent or delay the onset of a catalogue of appalling human afflictions – cancer, heart attacks, cardiovascular disease, Alzheimer's. Dolly already suggests we might soon have easy access to cloned replacement organs when our own pack up. If both happen then we'll all live much longer. Eventually we will expire, of course, but solely from frailty.

Source C

So long as one's economic situation is bearable, life in the so-called 'third age' can be rich, sometimes very rich. Mike Banks, albeit an ex-commando, describes vividly how he climbed the Old Man of Hoy in the Orkneys at 67 – and again at 71. Peter Preston, a former *Guardian* editor, writes of the joy of teaching his three-year-old grandson to use a computer. Pushpa Chaudhary, who fled India after partition, tells of the strength of her Asian community and the richness of her Hindu faith.

Question types 5, 6, 8 and 9

With reference to Sources A, B and C, summarise the views expressed about the changing status and roles of older people in our society. Assess the status and roles of older people in your own community and indicate how far you feel the current situation is satisfactory.   [50 marks]

Examiner's hints
- **Two questions** are being asked being asked and, although they are **linked**, it is important to demonstrate to the examiner that you have answered **both**.
- The **first question** is based on the skill of **summarising** the three sources, using the information and evidence in a **critical manner** to examine the views expressed about the changing role of older people in society.
- When **summarising**, it is important to make **brief references** to the sources to support an **argument** and to **avoid** re-writing large sections of the sources.
- The **second question** moves away from source evidence and seeks to focus on **your own community**. This means that clearly identified **local knowledge** is needed to **support the analysis**. You should aim to make answers to both questions of **roughly equal length**.
- There are marks available for all the Assessment Objectives but the **focus** is very much on **AO3**. 26 of the 50 marks will be awarded for showing that you can **select, interpret, evaluate and integrate information, evidence data and concepts to reach *reasoned conclusions***.

Answers can be found on pages 96–97.

ESSAY QUESTIONS

1 SHORT ESSAY ANSWERS

There is a skill in producing a short answer and it needs to be practised. Time is precious in the exam and examiners at A2 often report that candidates write too much when answering the type of questions below.

If only 3–5 marks are available, you should aim for a paragraph of continuous prose, highlighting key points. This is particularly important in some Edexcel questions.

Where 12 marks are available, as in question 3, your target should be 3–4 paragraphs, using prompts from the stimulus material. Even if your exam board does not set short essay questions, it is worthwhile looking through these as a source of ideas and as revision for the long essay answers you have to attempt at A2.

QUESTIONS AND STUDENT'S ANSWERS

Question type 10

1 Why do so many people think that there should be a close relationship between religious belief and moral behaviour? [3 marks]

RAVI'S ANSWER

It is obvious why there is a close relationship between religious belief and moral behaviour. There is a close connection between the values of a religion and the values that a person has in their normal life.

Question type 10

2 Explain how an artistic **or** architectural **or** literary **or** musical style arose in response to the period in which it developed. [5 marks]

RAVI'S ANSWER

Most young people like pop music. In the sixties when our parents were teenagers there were groups like the Stones and Beatles. It was a time of hippies, drugs and free love. Lots of changes have taken place since like punk, hip hop, garage, boy or girl bands. There is a lot of American influence and television plays its part when people can vote and make stars like Will Young and Gareth Gates.

How to score full marks

- Ravi's answers are both **short,** reflecting the relatively **small number of marks available** for the questions.

- In the answer to **question 1** he does not mention the possibility of **a non-believer** practising a moral code based on sensitivity to and concern for others. He might also have said that, for believers, religious belief is about the **relationship of humans to a divine being**.

- Although Ravi mentions the connection between religious and moral **values** in his answer to **question 1,** he needs to give supporting **examples** such as honesty.

- In his answer to **question 2**, Ravi chose pop music, mentioning several **different types**.

- Ravi's second answer does not always **link** the types of music with the response to the period in which they developed. He needs more **explicit points**, such as changing attitudes to authority, the role of new fashion trends, the greater spending power of teenagers and American/multi-cultural influences on popular music.

Question type 10

3 'In a global economy it is impossible to control the arms trade.' Discuss.   [12 marks]

CUT CONFLICT CAMPAIGN

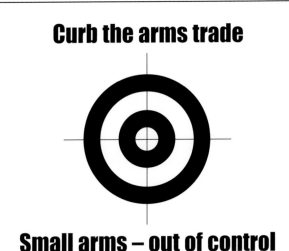

Curb the arms trade

Small arms – out of control

**'The indiscriminate use of weapons
has produced millions of refugees
and internally displaced people – and put in
peril relief personnel and their work.'**

**Source: Sergio Viera de Mello, Under Secretary General for
Humanitarian Affairs, October 1998**

ROHINTON'S ANSWER

There can be no doubt that we live in a global economy and that the sheer scale of this makes control very difficult. Globalisation has brought many problems and we often hear about threats to the environment.

In an ideal life we would be able to live more in peace and harmony but, across all the continents, wars are frequent. We know more about them because of 24 hours news programmes and satellite broadcasting so the horrors and violence come almost directly into our own home.

Wars need weapons and this is a sort of trade but often illegal. It is possible to buy guns on the streets of London. If that cannot be controlled, how can it be stopped across the world? Criminals will trade on evil. They have no morals. It is impossible to stop. So long as there are wars there will be an arms trade and misery, like Sergio Viera de Mello says. The world is too big a place to monitor this sort of trading and some governments are secretly involved.

$5/12$

How to score full marks

- There is not enough **discussion** in Rohinton's answer. Rohinton is **critical** of arms traders but he agrees that such trade is 'impossible to stop' without considering points like more effective customs check technology, better intelligence, legislation, greater public awareness and trade agreements among countries to work together.

- The essay questions used in Unit 5 of AQA Specification B all contain a small piece of **stimulus material**. Some of this can be used in the **framework** of your answer. Rohinton refers briefly to the Under Secretary General but fails to look at the extent to which the problem was 'out of control' or to mention refugees or dangers to relief personnel.

Don't forget ...

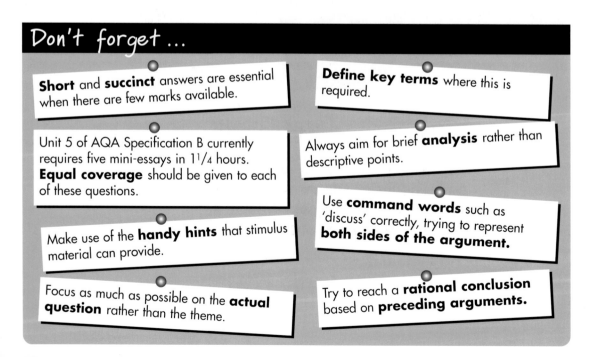

Short and **succinct** answers are essential when there are few marks available.

Define key terms where this is required.

Unit 5 of AQA Specification B currently requires five mini-essays in 1¼ hours. **Equal coverage** should be given to each of these questions.

Always aim for brief **analysis** rather than descriptive points.

Make use of the **handy hints** that stimulus material can provide.

Use **command words** such as 'discuss' correctly, trying to represent **both sides of the argument.**

Focus as much as possible on the **actual question** rather than the theme.

Try to reach a **rational conclusion** based on **preceding arguments.**

Question type 10

1 List the principles of aesthetic evaluation used to judge the quality of a work
of art **or** architecture **or** music **or** literature.   [4 marks]

2 Discuss whether we make 'the punishment fit the crime' when we commit
convicted criminals to prison.   [12 marks]

PRIME MINISTER'S PRISON VISIT

When the Prime Minister visited yesterday he mingled with
inmates who had improved their reading and writing, had taken a
maths exam while on remand, or were taking part in the jail's 'job
club'.

He was shown into the foundation English class where he sat at
a tiny plastic desk before hearing from the prisoners about their
experiences. In return he told them about the new 'custody of
work' scheme to help offenders get jobs on release.

Source: *The Guardian*, 27 February 2001

Examiner's hints
● Keep the word '**succinct**' in your mind. You can reach the maximum mark with a
short, perhaps very short, answer. No matter how well you continue after a
certain point, the examiner cannot award any extra marks after the maximum for
that question has been reached. You are losing valuable time that could be spent
on other parts of the exam paper. You may have to leave another question, with
higher marks, unfinished and this could have an adverse effect on your final
grade.

Answers can be found on pages 97–98.

2 LONG ESSAY ANSWERS

Long essays are a very common form of assessment at A2 and are compulsory in every specification, usually with at least 25 marks available for each. It is wise to spend at least 40 minutes on an answer. It is important to identify the key words in an essay, underlining them on the exam paper. You should almost certainly write a plan, but keep it brief. It is not sensible to think you can 'question spot' but it *is* a good idea to use previous A2 questions to sharpen your skills.

QUESTIONS AND STUDENTS' ANSWERS

Question type 11

1 'Voting should be compulsory in a democracy.'

Critically examine the arguments **for** and **against** this proposition.   [23 marks]

LAURA'S ANSWER

In this country voting is not compulsory. Nearly everyone over the age of 18 is entitled to vote and there are lots of opportunities to vote in local elections, elections for MPs and for the European Parliment. There was a General Election in 2001 and Labour won a big victory for the second time. Tony Blair remained Prime Minister and William Hague lost.

People do not have to vote if they do not want to, but the process is secret so nobody knows. Not as many people voted in 2001 as at previous elections in Britian. If voting was made compulsory more people would vote. People should vote if they want a say in how there country is run. In the past groups like the suffergettes fought hard to get women the vote and we should not take it for granted.

If voting was made compulsory how would you know who had voted and who hadn't? What would the penalties be if you didn't vote? That would not be popular. Voting is about freedom and people would want the right to choose to vote or not.

5/23

Laura's opening paragraph helps to 'set the scene'. She now needs to deal with the question's key issues.

Turnout (at 59%) was distinctly lower in the 2001 General Election than in preceding elections. Laura makes a couple of relevant points but they are not clearly expressed. The mis-spelling of 'Britain', like 'Parliament' is common.

Laura asks important questions but she should also be trying to answer them. The essay is very short and there is no real conclusion.

How to score full marks

- Use the first paragraph as a brief introduction, which displays some **knowledge** of the topic (compulsory voting) and the **concept** (a democracy). Laura might have mentioned the **falling turnout** in General Elections, dipping to below 60% in 2001, with much lower turnouts in local elections and elections for the European Parliament.

- Laura's second paragraph is sometimes **vague** and not always very **relevant.** There are also several **spelling mistakes** (e.g. 'Britian', 'there' instead of 'their' and 'suffergettes'). It would have been much more effective if she had covered points **for** compulsory voting, perhaps mentioning the need to ensure that citizens exercise their **responsibility** to vote.

- At all times, Laura needs to demonstrate that she can show the **particular skills** that are being tested. In this case, these are **AO3 skills** – *selecting, marshalling and interpreting a range of evidence and drawing conclusions.* (See Introduction page 6 for more details.)

- Laura needs to concentrate on the **arguments** for and against compulsory voting. She might have argued that voting in a democracy is a matter of **personal freedom**. She could also have said that, **in 'safe seats', voting can be a waste of time** unless voters support the candidate who appears to be a certain winner.

- Laura needs to write a **conclusion** based on arguments previously used, showing why she might support, or oppose, compulsory voting in a democracy. Because the range of **evidence** in Laura's essay is limited it is inevitable that the conclusion is difficult to identify, consequently keeping her in **Level 1** of the 20-mark range for AO3.

Don't forget ...

Always read the question carefully and pay close attention to the skills being tested. In this example, **20 marks** of the total of **23 test only Assessment Objective 3.** The other 3 marks are for **Assessment Objective 2,** which tests communication skills (see page 6).

Always try to draw your ideas together in a way that leads to a **logical** conclusion.

Make sure your answer is **balanced.** The case **for** and **against** compulsory voting in a democracy needs to be considered in detail on both sides.

Higher mark levels for this Edexcel question will be reached by including some **interpretation** of the **evidence** used. This will help to show your ability to think **critically** especially about the **reliability** of the evidence, which might be **factual, opinion-based** or a combination of the two.

2 'Although technology is able to solve some human problems and meet some needs, it creates even more problems and needs. We would therefore be better off without it.'

Critically evaluate this view from social, scientific and political perspectives.   [25 marks]

Leroy provides an effective opening, using examples and making a sound economics point.

More relevant examples but rather more a list than an effort to support the sort of synoptic question analysis required.

As the answer unfolds, it seems that Leroy is **describing** change rather than **evaluating** it from different perspectives.

Leroy has used the essay to praise the coming of several aspects of new technology but he has not taken a wider, more critical view based on the identification of some of its disadvantages.

LEROY'S ANSWER

Young people are used to growing up in a world of changing technology — flat screen televisions, multi-purpose mobile phones, sophisticated sound systems are but a few examples. In many cases, the micro-chip revolution and economies of scale in production have helped to cut prices so many electronic goods become cheaper.

Other examples of new technology can be found in medicine. Renal dialysis machines can help to keep patients alive, perhaps until a suitable donor is found for a transplant. DNA analysis can be used to trap 'cold case' murderers. MRI scanners, though expensive, provide doctors with the most detailed images to help them make the correct diagnosis.

Car technology has meant that driving is faster but safer. Cars are better designed and the introduction of things like air bags can reduce the impact of a traffic accident, ambulances and fire engines are better-equipped to deal with emergencies and, in Formula One racing, high speed crashes are less like to result in death because of improved technology.

I do not agree that we would be better off without new technology for the reasons stated. Leisure has been transformed for many people and life expectancy has gone up because people can have better treatment for illnesses or, if they are old, more effective boiler systems. Databases are far more effective than card index systems and spreadsheets have taken the place of ledgers. It is said that, within a few years, we will almost be able to get rid of books and newspapers. Perhaps there are some disadvantages in the fast pace of life today but if there is new technology we should try to get the best use out of it.

11/25

- Synoptic questions, usually found in parts of the Unit 6 exam papers, are difficult because they require knowledge which might link science, arts and the social sciences. In this context, Leroy starts well. He gives **examples** of changing **technology** and links them to **economics.**

- Leroy's second paragraph is quite effective but he needs a more **analytical framework** for his additional examples.

- The central weakness of Leroy's answer is clear by the end of paragraph 3 where **description** is used far more than the **critical analysis** required by the question. Having set out a few of the **benefits** of technology, Leroy needs to **contrast** these with some less desirable outcomes of new technology e.g. pollution, depletion of natural resources, financial costs.

- Leroy has tried to work to a **conclusion,** offering **some support for his arguments.** He might have tried to explore to the difficulties of **balancing good and less desirable outcomes.** He might also have conceded that the competitive side of **human nature** suggests that it is very unlikely that changes in technology will ever be stopped.

Don't forget ...

Synoptic essay questions found in Unit 6 test all four **Assessment Objectives** (see page 7). The breakdown for this 25 mark question is:

AO1 (relevant knowledge & understanding): 6 marks

AO2 (communication): 3 marks

AO3 (using evidence for analysis and drawing conclusions): 10 marks

AO4 (understanding of the different types of knowledge): 6 marks

The highest marks, particularly in synoptic essay questions, will go to candidates who use relevant **concepts** and show the ability to **reflect** on **different kinds of knowledge,** ideally drawing on points from science, the arts and social science. This might mean considering how, say, a scientist might use an **empirical approach** compared with a judgment about **aesthetics** by an artist.

REVISION NOTES

3 Drama on television and film is more popular than ever but relatively few people go to see live drama in the theatre. How do you explain this and what arguments would you use to encourage more people to experience live artistic performances? Refer to specific examples in your answer.

[25 marks]

LIAM'S ANSWER

Why don't I go to the theatre? It probably isn't very cool for most young people but the real problem is where I live. The nearest large town with a theatre is 40 miles away. I haven't yet passed my driving test. There are no trains and buses finish at 6 o'clock. To be completely honest, I'd feel a bit intimidated by the thought of dressing up. I sort of lack confidence in situations like that. Even if I could get a lift it's still a bit of a worry being in a city late at night. You can be an easy target for a mobile phone thief.

> The style is rather too personalised but there are some relevant points about proximity and access to theatres.

Is the effort of going to the theatre going to be worth it for somebody like me? I think not. There's a cinema nearby. Admittedly it's a bit primitive and doesn't get the best films but it's cheap and almost accessible. I'm not a great <u>Harry Potter</u> fan but you couldn't get those special effects at the theatre. I also saw <u>Saving Private Ryan</u> — another film with some amazing special effects. Too many cardboard cutouts in the theatre especially if, for you, the theatre's village hall stuff — the annual production of <u>My Fair Lady</u>. Amateur dramatics can be very amateurish.

> Liam's position is clear if not fully justified. Some supporting examples are used.

We live in an era of multi-channel TV, which offers a great deal of choice in the comfort of your own home. Subscription services like Sky can be costly but so can a trip to the theatre, as admission is often expensive. I know that the theatre is 'live' and if I lived in London, where some top actors and actresses like Nicole Kidman do theatre, I might have a different view. (Actually, if I did go to a live event in London it would probably be at <u>The Ministry of Sound</u>.)

> Liam might have looked in more detail at the qualities of 'live theatre'. His aside about **The Ministry of Sound** is one that might be shared by many of his peers.

Assuming that the case for attending live performances can be made — maybe a pop concert — I'd obviously have to look for a magic wand. One that will provide better transport and lower admission prices for sixth formers. Tastes change. People would rather see <u>Eastenders</u> several nights a week on their TV screen. Colour, pace, action and good actors. More dramatic than the theatre.

15/25

How to score full marks

- Liam starts by asking a question. This can be a risky strategy because it can lead to too many **rhetorical questions** and not enough time being spent **answering** the question asked. He avoids this pitfall and, in fact, uses the opening question effectively.

- Liam's style is rather **personalised** and this can lead to too many **anecdotal points** ('I think', 'I believe' – Liam uses 'I' six times in the first paragraph). He does not quite get the balance right between **individual ideas** and more **detached** and **objective** analysis.

- The second paragraph is a little too **dismissive**. Local and regional theatre productions can be of high quality.

- **The strengths** of Liam's answer are the **clarity** of his **communication** and his ability to provide some **supporting examples.** A **weakness** is that he says relatively little about the second part of the question on how to encourage people to experience live artistic performances. He might have discussed **more emphasis on the arts in education, better publicity,** or the **wider use of subsidies.**

Don't forget ...

Avoid an **over-personalised response in essays.**

There are few marks for **posing** questions and leaving possible answers unexplored.

Supporting examples are very important. The wording of questions often makes it clear that examples are required but a major weakness of many candidates is that they do not provide **a range of *relevant* examples** when answering essay questions.

Examiners do not necessarily reserve the highest marks for a **'safe'** answer or a **defence of the status quo.** Providing it is backed by **analysis** and **evidence**, a **bold and imaginative style** can be very effective.

Question type 11

1 Britain is one of the windiest areas in Europe and could obtain a significant contribution to electricity from wind turbines.

Explain how a wind turbine can be used to generate electricity.

Discuss the benefits and disadvantages of this means of electricity generation.

[25 marks]

2 Should public utilities such as electricity, gas and water supplies, or public services such as buses, trains, postal and telephone systems, remain in private ownership? What are the strengths and weaknesses of private enterprise providing vital services?

[25 marks]

3 To what extent can humanism act as a substitute for religion in everyday life?

[50 marks]

Examiner's hints
- Essays need a brief introduction, clear arguments with examples and a conclusion which sums up the main points without repeating too many of them.
- Use reasoned arguments rather than assertions, opinions and sweeping statements.

Answers to question 1 can be found on pages 98–99.

3 REPORT WRITING/PROBLEM SOLVING EXERCISES

The report writing examples used are taken specifically from AQA Specification B, Unit 4. Other specifications do not test report writing but the analytical skills are transferable to other types of source-based questions.

'Problem solving' is a common feature of A2 questions, sometimes using data and often featuring in essays. In mathematics there is usually an answer to a problem. In other areas – particularly in society, politics and economics – there is no single solution. The skill lies in being able to identify several policy options that could be tried. Often it is a chance to show that you can think in a more objective way, perhaps recognising your personal feelings but trying to take a wider, more strategic view. You will also be able to gain AO4 marks (see page 6) by showing that you recognise the limitations of knowledge and its applications.

QUESTION AND STUDENT'S ANSWER

Source 13: ECOLOGY, CONSERVATION AND TOURISM IN THE GALAPAGOS ISLANDS

Read the following passage and complete the task below.

Oil on troubled waters

The oil spill from an ageing tanker in the Galapagos is small by global pollution standards. More birds and wildlife will die on UK roads in one day than in the Galapagos because of the spill. But several things make the spill unique. About a third of the islands' 600 or so native plant species are found only there. Of the 57 species of reptiles, land birds and mammals, more than 80% are found nowhere else. The spill may be small, but so is the archipelago. Its surrounding seas are as much part of its ecology as the land itself. Most of the islands' animals depend on the sea for their food, directly or indirectly.

Charles Darwin called the Galapagos 'a little world within itself' and his observations of its flora and fauna helped to formulate his theory of evolution. Since then, the 19 islands and 42 islets have become a symbol of ecological vulnerability and unique plant and animal life. 97% of this land and surrounding seas are protected and there are teams of professional scientists and conservationists working around the clock to save it.

Yet this spill is just the latest in a long line of threats. There have been dreadful droughts when thousands of animals have died of starvation. But more influential to the islands' ecology has been man. Settlers brought domestic animals such as dogs and cats as well as black rats. Dogs kill tortoises; rats kill every hatchling.

Meanwhile, tourism and fishing have wrought havoc with the marine environment. Sea turtles have died from swallowing plastic, tossed overboard from cruise ships; sea lions have their muzzles cut by tin cans that have fallen to the sea bed. Visitors bring seeds, spores and insects on their clothes and shoes. Strict laws are in place, but they are not always enforced.

Tourism took off in the 1960s, encouraged by the Ecuador government's need for foreign currency to service its massive debt. Its growth led to an increase in immigration from the mainland; most immigrants have turned to the sea for work. The fishing industry demands greater lobster and shark quotas from the 7m hectare marine park. The islands are now the richest part of Ecuador.

Source: *Guardian Unlimited,* **24 January 2001**

Question types 1, 3, 6, 8, 9 and 12

Imagine that you are a scientist reporting to the Ecuador government on the future of the Galapagos.

Produce a report which communicates:

(a)	details of the nature of the problems in the Galapagos	[15 marks]
(b)	what you consider to be the responsibilities of the different parties involved	[15 marks]
(c)	what measures should be taken to prevent these problems happening again.	[20 marks]

A further ten marks will be awarded for communicating in a concise and logical way in a form appropriate to report writing. [10 marks]

JANE'S ANSWER

(a) There is an oil pollution threat resulting from spillage from a sunken tanker. Internationally it is a relatively small problem, but there are problems that are specific to the Galapagos where the seas are very important to ecological life.

In the nineteenth century, Charles Darwin used the plant life of the island to help develop his theory of evolution. He referred to the Galapagos as 'a little world within itself' and much of the plant and animal life is unique to the islands. This makes such life very vulnerable and marine pollution is not the only threat — drought provided another example.

Perhaps, though, it is man and the animals he brought to the islands that pose the biggest threat to the ecology. The animals threaten the breeding cycle of tortoises and industry brings problems as well as benefits. Tourism is important to the local economy but tins and plastic are dangerous to marine life. Laws to prevent contaminants like spores on the clothes and shoes of tourists are not easily enforced.

Economic and scientific problems are inextricably linked. Fishing is one industry that can help to reduce government debt but fishermen seek to land higher and higher numbers of fish. Over the longer term this may threaten the breeding cycle and have a significant impact on the numbers of shark and lobster.

13/15

> Jane makes an excellent start, summarising a range of issues. She is aware of both short- and longer-term implications and writes in a clear effective manner.

(b) The difficulties outlined should not be assigned to one group. Conservationists will clearly have protection of the environment and wildlife uppermost in their mind. The government is responsible for ensuring that there are laws to offer protection to species that are threatened. Multinational companies should be prepared to show responsibility. Those who run industries in the Galapagos should be reminded that short-term profits can have wider consequences. Tourists will need to take more care and show responsibility, especially where litter is not biodegradable. If they don't, the islands may soon cease to be the richest part of Ecuador.

6/15

> Jane does well to identify so many interested groups but she really needs to add a little more on each of them.

(c) It is unrealistic to think that the Galapagos can once again become an undeveloped country or that scientists can produce miracle solutions to the problems of marine pollution or shortages caused by over-fishing.

Strict laws with compensation should be brought in to prevent oil spillages, perhaps on an international basis.

Ecologists and those involved in scientific research must ensure that their work is given greater publicity so that more people are aware of the problem.

Tourism needs to be more closely regulated. If there are fishing quotas perhaps there should be tourist quotas.

Governments need to recognise that there are long-term consequences of actions that threaten unique plant and animal life.

7/20

Communication 7/10

Total 33/60

How to score full marks

- Jane's answer to (**a**) is **well written** and **informative**. She **uses information from the extract** effectively and produced a **clear summary** of the problems in the Galapagos.

- Her response to (**b**) is **much shorter** even though both parts of the question are worth 15 marks. Consequently, though she **identifies the different parties,** her answer **lacks a more detailed consideration** of their **responsibilities** and **relative positions**.

- In (**b**) she might have said a little about conservationists taking a more **pro-active role**, perhaps forming/involving **pressure groups**. More could have been said about **government law enforcement** or *how* multi-nationals might show more responsibility or the sort of steps that could be taken to remind industrialists and tourists of their respective responsibilities.

- There were 20 marks for (**c**) yet the answer is also **too short**. The points that Jane makes all have relevance and potential but each needs an additional sentence or two to give more **depth** and **coherence**. (What the implications of a tourist quota might be for the economy and whether, in practical terms, it would be a realistic option.)

- There are 10 additional marks for '**communicating in a concise and logical way**'. Despite variations in her style she presents ideas and information in a **structured manner free from errors of punctuation, spelling and grammar.**

Don't forget ...

One hour is allowed to complete this AQA Specification B Unit 4 examination paper. There are 15–20 marks for the three parts of the exercise. Try to spend **equal time** on each part.

Use language, style and structure appropriate to **report writing.** The style should be **detached** and **balanced.** Ten additional marks are allowed for appropriate **communication skills,** so a good and accurate written style can gain you marks.

Keep the **assessment objectives** in mind. Examiners will be looking for evidence of **knowledge & understanding, critical analysis** and **evaluation & interpretation** (see page 6).

Try to practise **problem solving skills.** The subject matter is less important than the ability to see **both sides of a question** and the ability to grasp how problems might be **resolved** in a **realistic and effective** way.

Always seek to make a distinction between **facts** and **opinions.**

Do not be afraid to emphasise the **difficulties of conflict resolution.** Most problems are more difficult than they seem. **Compromise** is not always easy to reach and may not satisfy the parties concerned. There is merit in recognising this and showing why some problems are **so difficult to resolve.**

Source 14: INDUSTRIAL RELATIONS IN THE MINING INDUSTRY

1   Read the following passage and complete the tasks below.

Strike closes pit in 'silly' dispute

In what must rate as one of the most bizarre industrial disputes, a coal mine owned by its workforce was closed by a strike. Around a hundred miners at the last deep pit in Wales, Tower Colliery, walked out after a row with managers who told two employees to change their work schedule.

The colliery became a workers' co-operative about five years ago. When it was put up for sale in 1995, after British Coal said it should close, 239 of the pit's workers chipped in £8000 each from their redundancy money and kept it open. Tower was traditionally one of the most militant collieries in Britain – absolute solidarity made a picket line unnecessary during the strike of 1984–1985.

The latest trouble surfaced when coalface workers were told that they would be transferred to another part of the pit. They refused, prompting a walkout by the morning shift. Officials for the National Union of Mineworkers urged miners who were due to clock on for the afternoon shift to work normally, but they also decided to strike. Tyrone O'Sullivan, a director of the co-operative and former NUM official, said: 'This is the first time muscles have been flexed since we took over. Under British Coal there would have been an agreement to enable work to continue'.

Mr O'Sullivan said that production had stopped, although coal already brought to the surface was being delivered to customers. He added that the two workers had been told to do jobs they were trained to do, but they refused and then decided to go home.

The survival of Tower is important in an area largely untouched by the electronics era. Unemployment in the valley is around 10% and health and housing problems abound. It is estimated that without the colliery the local economy would lose up to £10m a year.

Source: *Guardian Unlimited,* 12 April 2000

Imagine you are an independent consultant reporting to the co-operative.

Produce a report on the incident which communicates:

(a) details of the problems encountered at the colliery [15 marks]

(b) which parties you consider to be responsible for the problems
and why [15 marks]

(c) what recommendations you would make to minimise the risk of a
recurrence. [20 marks]

A further ten marks will be awarded for communicating in a concise and
logical way in a form appropriate to report writing. [10 marks]

Examiner's hints
- Your central task is to produce a report and it is vital that you try to do so in a
  way that is both **detached and analytical**. There are a lot of marks to aim
  for and there are three sections of the report to complete. Try to **divide your
  time equally**, thus avoiding a very long section and one that is very short.
- Remember that up to 10 marks are awarded 'for communicating in a *concise* and
  logical manner'.

Answers can be found on pages 99–101.

Source-based questions are used in all the specifications at A2. Some students think that such questions are easy because 'the answers are in the source'. The *information* is there to help provide a framework for your answer but you need to show the ability to build on the source and to think critically about it.

QUESTION AND STUDENT'S ANSWER

Question types 6, 8, 9 and 11

Source 15: THE ETHNIC UNDERCLASS?

Read this passage and answer the question that follows.

The Ethnic Underclass?

While some ethnic minorities are doing very well in Britain, black and Asian people often face a series of disadvantages and poorer life chances that their white counterparts do not encounter. Pakistanis, Bangladeshis and Afro-Caribbeans, in particular, face a series of disadvantages in Britain compared with the white majority, although there are differences within each group.

● Afro-Caribbeans, Pakistanis and Bangladeshis are less likely than white people to secure the best jobs. These groups are under-represented in non-manual occupations, particularly in management and professional work. They are hugely under-represented in parliament and the top elite occupations.

● They are over-represented in semi-skilled and unskilled manual occupations, and often work longer and more unsociable hours (shift work and night work) than white people.

● Black and Asian people are less likely to be employed when competing with whites with the same qualifications for the same job.

● Black and Asian people have lower average earnings, even when they have the same job level as white people. Small-scale surveys have shown that male Afro-Caribbeans earn 15% less, and Asians 18% less, than whites. Ethnic minority groups are far more likely to be in the poorest fifth of the population.

- People from ethnic minorities are more likely to face unemployment, especially those of Afro-Caribbean and Pakistani/Bangladeshi origin.

- Skilled and experienced ethnic minority women are twice as likely as white women to be unemployed, according to the Equal Opportunities Commission. Black and Asian women frequently work longer hours in poor conditions than white women or men, and receive roughly 75% of white women's pay, even though they are on average better educated.

Source: Ken Browne

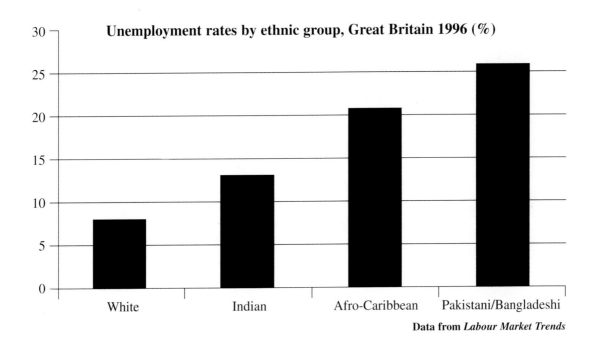

Unemployment rates by ethnic group, Great Britain 1996 (%)

Data from *Labour Market Trends*

'We shall only secure the benefits of cultural diversity if members of ethnic minorities have the same job opportunities as the white majority.'

Bearing in mind

- educational
- political
- legal
- economic

limits to what can be done, how might we ensure that ethnic minorities do not form a socio-economic underclass in Britain? [40 marks]

DION'S ANSWER

We are increasingly aware that Britain is becoming a more culturally diverse country and there are often disputes about job opportunities. Despite acts to make discrimination on grounds of race illegal, it is still believed that white people have better access to jobs and the graph in the question proves this.

The facts speak for themselves. The first bullet point says 'Afro-Caribbeans, Pakistanis, and Bangladeshis are less likely to secure the best jobs.' The jobs they get are much more likely to be less skilled with lower wages. The fourth bullet point provides evidence for this. 'Ethnic minority groups are far more likely to be in the poorest fifth of the population.' It also says that people from ethnic minorities are more likely to face unemployment.

In the area where I live there is a lot of disagreement about which groups get the best jobs and help from the council. Unemployment is high for most groups, especially since more asylum seekers came to the area. This has put a great strain on the services and most people live on benefits rather than getting jobs. Perhaps if a law cut the number of asylum seekers, more people of all races would have more chance. In politics, the British National Party does not believe in a multi-cultural society.

Part of the trouble is in the schools. Not enough is done for those from ethnic minorities, especially those who are unable to speak English very well. They fall behind quickly and are soon labelled as trouble makers. Perhaps they are discouraged by the fact that they are more likely to end up unemployed.

The British National Party seems to want to go back to the past when there were few non-white people. It might have been like that years ago but things have changed. It would be no solution to the problems of 2002. Everyone needs better training for jobs in subjects like IT. In our area, a lot of the old factory jobs have gone and won't come back. Above all it's important for schools to tackle discrimination as early as primary schools. We can never get rid of prejudice. It's human nature. But we can try to show what it's like to have fewer chances because of the colour of your skin.

16/40

Quite a promising introduction until Dion claims that the bar chart **proves** his point. It does not. It only shows that, in 1996, the proportion of white people unemployed was lower than the proportion of certain other ethnic groups.

Dion is relying too much on material that forms part of the question. He is also not focusing on the key issue of what might be done to tackle some of the issues that he has raised.

Local knowledge and evidence can often be useful but Dion's account is largely anecdotal. There is a danger that asylum seekers become a scapegoat for wider social and economic problems.

This point has potential but Dion does not identify measures such as additional language support, which could be used in a positive way.

This is probably the best part of Dion's answer because he is identifying things that might be done to reduce the chances of ethnic minorities forming a socio-economic underclass. However, these points would have had more effect if they had come at an earlier stage.

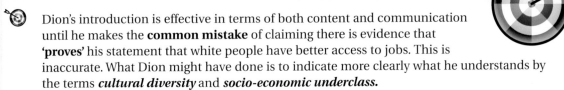

🎯 Dion's introduction is effective in terms of both content and communication until he makes the **common mistake** of claiming there is evidence that **'proves'** his statement that white people have better access to jobs. This is inaccurate. What Dion might have done is to indicate more clearly what he understands by the terms *cultural diversity* and *socio-economic underclass.*

🎯 Questions based on a **source** often provide useful material for the answer. **Facts,** contrary to what Dion claims, do *not* necessarily 'speak for themselves'. They require **critical examination** and **interpretation.** Dion's second paragraph is largely wasted. The evidence, taken from the source, is not really used in a way that is relevant to the question.

🎯 Good clues are to be found in the **bullet points.** Answers to the **synoptic questions** found in Unit 6 require knowledge and evidence drawn from **several different areas of General Studies.** This is reflected only in parts of Dion's last three paragraphs.

🎯 In the main part of his essay, Dion needs to **focus more extensively** on what might be done to reduce the possibilities of ethnic minorities becoming an underclass. He might have included points such as inner city initiatives, tackling racial stereotypes and 'institutional racism', improved careers advice, immigration policies, employment training and language policies which might make more people aware of benefits to which they are entitled.

🎯 Another clue in the question might have helped with the conclusion. Candidates are advised to bear in mind **'limits to what can be done'.** We should not expect, no matter how great our knowledge and experience, that there will *always* be ways of saying that we can *ensure* that a particular policy will work.

Don't forget ...

Synoptic questions, found in the Unit 6 papers of the different examining groups, are the most difficult of all A2 questions to answer. They are *synoptic* in the sense that they require knowledge **from most areas of General Studies** and that represents a much **wider range** than other A level subjects (see page 7).

Do not be afraid to explore **concepts** and to try to explain them at an early point in your answer.

Use your **own knowledge** and **evidence provided by the source** when answering a source-based question. Do not over-rely on what the source provides and do not use it simply to **describe** a situation. Synoptic questions usually call for a higher level of **analysis** and **evaluation.** (Not *what happened* but *why* it might have happened and what the *possible consequences* of a course of action might be.)

Always be prepared to accept the **limitations** of what might be achievable. Assessment Objective 4, a common feature of synoptic questions, is not only about **different kinds of knowledge.** It also covers the **limitations** of knowledge.

Source 16: PRESSURE GROUPS AND DIRECT ACTION

Read the passage below, which considers the activities of pressure groups who are opposed to the use of animals for scientific research and to other things that they consider to be a threat to people or the government. Answer the question at the end of the passage in the form of an essay.

Pressure groups and direct action

Pity anyone still involved, however remotely, with Huntingdon Life Sciences. The company, which tests animals for the pharmaceutical industry, has been under extreme physical and financial siege for several years. Exposed on TV and in this newspaper for its treatment of puppies, it has been taken to court and heavily fined, told to clean up its act by the government, seen its share price drop to an all-time low and its scientists vilified and threatened. Its major shareholder, the financial house Phillips and Drew, has received bomb threats and now the remaining investors are not just being targeted by individual letter, but by personal protest outside their homes.

This week attention turned to the formerly anonymous David Braybrook, a pensioner aged 70. Like 1700 investors, he had been sent a letter some months ago by the British Union for the Abolition of Vivisection Reform Group. Unless he sold his shares within a week, he was told, he was liable to have his home picketed. Mr Braybrook did nothing. He opened his door to be met by a crowd of protestors including a man dressed as a beagle.

The protest was short, sharp, peaceful and made its point. Braybrook, clearly shocked, had a series of 2 metre tall photographs, showing animal cruelty at Huntingdon Life Sciences some years ago, plastered across the walls of his house and underwent a separate ordeal by press. By yesterday, the protestors had moved on.

There are now promises to expand the campaign to other Huntingdon investors. A spokesman said: 'This was the first in a series of demonstrations. We will be circulating the names and addresses of shareholders to other independent groups and we hope they will be starting their own protests.' Taking protest to individuals is not new but taking it to anonymous members of the public, rather than corporate chiefs or government ministers, is.

By the 1980s, environment, consumer, human rights and animal rights campaigners were increasingly frustrated. They changed tack. One of the tactics was to buy shares in companies, attend annual meetings in force and cause mayhem or deep embarrassment by asking awkward questions of the board of directors. But in the 1990s, direct action by individuals came of age, first at Twyford Down and then at Newbury. Environmentalists had no hesitation in naming names and exposing directors and government officials responsible for what they saw as destructive road-building policies.

Malcolm Walker, the head of Iceland foods, started the corporate flight from genetically modified foods. Walker received six letters asking him what he was going to do about the novel foods and was intrigued because he had not even heard of genetic modification. Almost as soon as he found out, he asked his technical director to steer clear of them. Meanwhile, ethical investments were becoming increasingly important, largely because of personal lobbying of groups and individuals. But in the past few years, the pressure to act in a socially and ethically responsible way has been turning to anyone who deals in money.

Jonathan Porritt, having run Friends of the Earth in the 1980s, has seen the money protests develop over 20 years and has long campaigned to make the City more ethical. 'People don't like their names in lights. They're more sensitive now, more open to the impact on their reputations. I suspect that the sort of protests against Huntingdon, the personalising of protest, will become much more common.'

'This is the logical extension of direct action protest,' says Tony Juniper, policy director of Friends of the Earth. 'The City is an important bastion, a source of enormous power that campaigners and activists have not been able to influence very much. Most people have a stake in the City through their pension or insurance funds. But it's not the City's money, it's ours. This sort of protest turns faceless people into individuals.'

But the companies and industries that have been targeted are also appealing to higher authority. In the past few months, the pharmaceutical industry has called on the government to have legislation to clamp down on what it calls 'economic terrorism'. Huntingdon itself has written to Tony Blair urging him to bring 'extremist animal rights groups' within the remit of terrorist legislation. The City, too, has welcomed the massive police attention being paid to groups such as Reclaim the Streets which is planning to hold a weekend of protest over May Day which may include action against City institutions.

Yesterday, Braybrook was unrepentant, and becoming something of a hero for the City, which likes people not to bow to pressure. 'I won't have a man dressed as a beagle making up my mind for me,' he told reporters. 'I am at liberty to buy what I like and it is my intention to leave the money where it is.'

Adapted from 'This time it's personal' by John Vidal,
***The Guardian* 12 April 2000**

How far is it possible to justify direct action, which may include breaking the law, by individuals and pressure groups opposing scientific and other activities with which they disagree?

[50 marks]

Examiner's hints
- Do not make the common mistake of simply re-writing the source in summary form. That will only provide descriptive material that will gain you few marks.
- You will need to read the source quite quickly so it might pay to make a short summary plan of the main points. Label it clearly as a plan but do not cross it out. The examiner might find something to reward.
- Become used to reading articles of a similar length from the newspapers. Choose a topic that is part of the specification you are studying. Compare some articles and think critically about what they do, and do not, tell you.
- Look particularly for 'synoptic' articles combining elements of the arts, technology and social sciences.
- With any sort of longer essay, make sure you have practised 'writing against the clock' for 40 minutes. It should be an essential part of your preparation for A2.

Answers can be found on pages 101–102.

1 FOREIGN LANGUAGE COMPREHENSION

In A2 General Studies the testing of knowledge and understanding in a foreign language is specific to **AQA Specification A**. It tests your ability to negotiate, understand broadly or interpret with accuracy, **one** of the three major European languages, **French, German** or **Spanish**. It appears as the first of two questions in **Unit 4 (Culture, Morality, Arts and Humanities)** where the second is an essay (**one** from a choice of six questions). In each language there will be between four and six separate passages, each on a different everyday theme or topic, and a total of 20–25 multiple choice questions **in English**. Your choice of language must be made when you make your entry for the examination. The example questions given here involve only **French**, but the general advice is valid for all three languages. For German and Spanish examples you need to look at past papers.

QUESTIONS AND ANSWERS

Read the information given below. For each of the four questions that follow, choose the answer you consider the best of the alternatives **A**, **B**, **C** or **D**.

Sets of four questions like this are quite common and it is a matter of **picking out the relevant bit of detail** from each one **that matches** the question. You can tell **from the title** that they are all **brief descriptions** of films being shown on the television that evening.

LES FILMS TÉLÉVISÉS DE CE SOIR

A 23h 05 TF1	**Tout feu, tout flamme**	**B** 18h 40 la5ª	**Le gorille vous salue bien**
Charme, humour et élégance avec ce film de Jean-Paul Rappeneau (*La vie de château, Le sauvage*) qui voit s'opposer un père, Yves Montand, et sa fille, Isabelle Adjani, jeune fille décidée et trop sérieuse. Le père se conduit en adolescent, la fille est bien trop adulte pour son âge. Délicieux, très drôle et très tendre.		De l'espionnage «bien de chez nous» dans la tradition française des années 50-60, façon Monocle ou Lemmy Caution. Lino Ventura y trouvait son premier rôle de vedette et y gagnait d'emblée la sympathie du public.	
C 22h 45 M8	**Ticks**	**D** 23h 40 3	**Le chemin des écoliers**
De la pure série B, dotée de faibles moyens financiers mais d'une bonne volonté évidente: les méchants sont des tiques géantes qui s'attaquent à un groupe de jeunes campeurs. Les amateurs de rossignols réjouissants y trouveront leur compte.		Spécialiste de la comédie légère, Michel Boisrond se lançait dans la satire de moeurs en nous montrant le comportement de deux générations dans la capitale occupée par les Allemands. Rien de sérieux là-dedans: il s'agit de faire sourire avant tout.	

Which of the four films (**A** to **D**) described above

1 launched the career of its star?

2 is set in Paris during the Second World War?

3 shows an adult and a child acting strangely?

4 was made on a limited budget?

Vocabulary

se conduire	to behave
doté	endowed
comportement	behaviour

Read the following article and answer **Questions 5 to 8**.

This second sequence of five questions is based on an article about holiday language courses for students of English, but with a difference. Again the information for these is **in the title**, and in **skimming the article** to **understand the gist** of it. There are no formal classroom activities – the course is about the students planning and arranging their own holiday tour.

LES RAIDS LINGUISTIQUES, DES VACANCES INTELLIGENTES
Associer cours de langue, culture, tourisme et sport est un excellent moyen d'améliorer son anglais.

Avec ses cours de grammaire et de vocabulaire, le séjour linguistique classique d'une ou deux semaines ne fait pas toujours recette auprès des ados. Apprendre l'anglais d'accord, mais pas de façon scolaire ! Pour répondre à leur attente, il existe des raids linguistiques: trois semaines de voyage en bus dans une région touristique d'Angleterre, d'Irlande ou d'Ecosse. Avec tous les matins de la première semaine, des cours de langue basés sur la préparation du périple.

L'anglais en voyageant
Dans ce séjour nomade, les progrès sont au rendez-vous. Se déplacer dans le pays, utiliser l'anglais pour faire ses courses ou le plein d'essence du minibus, louer une planche à voile, discuter de musique avec un prof pendant le trajet … sont de bons moyens de se débloquer à l'oral. Un ado préfère parler de sujets qu'il aime plutôt que rabâcher des verbes irréguliers! D'autant que les adultes qui accompagnent le raid sont aussi là pour corriger les fautes. La décontraction n'empêche pas le sérieux!

La première semaine, en préparant leur périple, en traduisant le guide de leur prochain voyage, les jeunes révisent leur grammaire, apprennent le vocabulaire du camping, des sports qu'ils vont pratiquer, etc. Logés pendant cette période en famille d'accueil ou en pension, ils conversent et découvrent d'autres habitudes.

Culture et sport se complètent
Maîtriser une langue, c'est aussi connaître le pays. En visitant châteaux, musées, sites naturels et historiques, l'ado acquiert une culture générale utile en anglais comme en histoire/geo.

Ces journées culturelles alternent avec des journées sportives de détente. Équitation, VTT, tennis, planche à voile, natation, randonnées … L' ado profite de vacances équilibrées, aussi instructives que ludiques.

Vocabulary

raid	trek	*se débloquer*	to loosen one's tongue
ados	adolescents	*VTT = vélo tout terrain*	mountain bike
périple	tour, route	*ludique*	sporting
rabâcher	to recite		

5 The article describes language courses that last

   A one week

   B two weeks

   C three weeks

   D four weeks

6 The first week is spent

   A travelling around the country

   B planning the itinerary

   C discussing music with the teachers

   D getting to know the guide for the trip

7 Which type of accommodation is **not** mentioned in the article?

   A youth hostels

   B boarding houses

   C host families

   D camping

8 Each of the following activities is mentioned **except**

   A swimming

   B climbing

   C cycling

   D walking

Read the following article and answer **Questions 9 to 12**.

The theme for this last sequence of six questions is once again to be found **in the title** *Génération bricoleuses* ('A generation of handywomen'). Note that this key word is **given in the vocabulary**.

GÉNÉRATION BRICOLEUSES

Ponceuses, perceuses et autres scies sont enfin tombées entre les mains des femmes.
Et les fabricants font tout pour les séduire.

Conscients d'avoir une nouvelle clientèle à conquérir, les magasins de bricolage redoublent d'ingéniosité et axent leur politique commerciale vers les femmes. Comment les attirer alors? Pour Benoit Vermesch, directeur marketing chez Castorama, «les femmes souhaitent davantage de sécurité. Elles veulent également des outils de qualité, pratiques, simples à utiliser, légers et maniables. Si en plus ils peuvent être beaux, sans ressembler à des outils 'Barbie', c'est gagné.» Il fallait donc offrir aux femmes un lieu engageant où elles se repèrent facilement. Résultat, pour répondre à ces attentes, les anciennes «halles à outils» se transform: on y pénètre maintenant souvent par des rayons décoration où l'on peut glaner quelques idées au passage, puis le petit bricolage, pour arriver tout doucement vers le gros outillage.

Stages, magazines et fiches pratiques

A l'occasion du dernier salon Créations et Savoir-faire, Castorama a même lancé un nouveau label : Castorama pour elles. Mais ce n'est pas tout, la plupart des enseignes ont maintenant leur magazine, proposent des fiches conseils et même des stages de formation gratuits, le samedi matin. Mais pourquoi les femmes sont-elles si nombreuses à succomber aux charmes de la perceuse? La raison première est économique: entreprendre des travaux coûte cher. Alors les femmes «s'y collent». Plus question de dépendre d'un mari pas forcément disponible. Sans oublier qu'elles sont aussi nombreuses à vivre seules et doivent donc faire face à des tâches qui étaient autrefois l'apanage des hommes. Et c'est plutôt bien: «Ce regard féminin est bon pour tous, il permet de faire évoluer un matériel qui ne bougeait plus beaucoup et, qui sait, peut-être aurons-nous un jour des espaces pour les femmes», se plaît à imaginer B. Vermesch.

Vocabulary			
bricoleuse	good at DIY	*maniable*	easy to handle
ponceuse	sander	*se repérer*	to find your way round
scie	saw	*glaner*	to pick up
séduire	to seduce	*enseignes*	brand names
apanage	prerogative	*disponible*	available
outils	tools		

9 DIY manufacturers are targeting female customers by

  A giving tools away

  B employing twice as many saleswomen

  C making tools look like toys

  D responding to their needs

10 Each of the following is a factor when persuading women to buy tools **except**

  A weight

  B manageability

  C price

  D simplicity

11 DIY stores have been made more attractive to women by

  A making their layout less confusing

  B selling 'Barbie' dolls

  C reducing the amount of waiting time at the checkout

  D asking them for their ideas

12 More women are taking up DIY because

   1   they want to save money

   2   there is no one else around to do it

   3   their husbands show little interest

   4   they are forced into it by their husbands

   Answer

   A **1** alone is true

   B **1** and **2** only are true

   C **1**, **2** and **3** only are true

   D All of them are true

How to score full marks

Question	Correct answer	Examiner's hints
1	B	The **vital detail** for 'launched the career of its star' is in the final sentence of B: *Lino Ventura y trouvait son premier rôle de vedette* … (= first starring role) in a spy film in the style of those made in France during the 1950s.
2	D	This is to be found in D, which describes 'a light-hearted comedy satirising the behaviour of two different generations *dans la capitale occupée par les Allemands* …' – the capital (Paris) occupied by the German forces (during the Second World War).
3	A	Film A is about the 'conflict between (*s'opposer*) a father and his single-minded daughter (*décidée et trop sérieuse*) where the father *se conduit en adolescent* (behaves like an adolescent) and the daughter *est bien trop adulte pour son âge* (much too adult for her age)'.
4	C	If you have worked out the first three correctly, then the answer should be C. This time the **vital clue** is in the first sentence 'a pure B movie, *dotée de faibles moyens financiers* … = (literally) endowed with limited (weak) financial means'.
5	C	The key detail is in the first paragraph '*des raids linguistiques: trois semaines de voyage en bus* … (= language 'treks': three weeks travelling by bus …)'.
6	B	This follows straightforwardly when you find the **key phrase** '*La première semaine* (the first week), *en préparant leur périple* (preparing their route) …' This points to answer B. Note **essential words** which you might not be expected to know from your GCSE work are included in the **vocabulary list**.
7	A	For this type of question you must **identify the equivalent French words** that are in the text, in order to isolate the one that is not. In this case, towards the end of the third paragraph you have *camping … en famille d'accueil* (host family) … *en pension* (boarding house) but no mention of youth hostels.
8	B	This question requires an identical process. **Find the equivalent French words** that are there to identify the one which is not. These are in the activities mentioned at the end of the passage: *Équitation* (horse riding), *VTT* (mountain biking), *tennis, planche à voile* (sail boarding), *natation* (swimming), *randonnées* (walking) …' The answer **not** included is B (climbing).

Question	Correct answer	Examiner's hints
9	D	'Responding to the needs of female customers' is the **theme of the sub-title** '*Et les fabricants font tout pour les séduire*' (and the manufacturers are doing everything to attract them) and the whole of the first paragraph. **Other clues** are to be found in the middle of the paragraph in *offrir aux femmes un lieu engageant où elles se repèrent facilement* (an inviting place where they can easily find their way around) and *pour répondre à ces attentes …* (to respond to these expectations … *attendre* = to expect, as well as to wait).
10	C	The word for tools is **given in the vocabulary** (*outils*) and what women want in tools is set out in the list early in the first paragraph '*Elles veulent également des outils de qualité, pratiques, simples à utiliser, légers et maniables* (They want tools of good quality, practical, simple to use, light and easy to handle)'. Of the alternatives given, price is the exception, the one **not** mentioned.
11	A	The **last sentence of the first paragraph** is about the change in the layout of the stores and the logical order in which different sections are now set out to appeal more to women (*… pour répondre à ces attentes*), moving from the household decoration shelves (*des rayons décoration*) and suggestions for ideas to try out as you walk through (*où l'on peut glaner quelques idées au passage*), to small DIY jobs (*le petit bricolage*) and eventually through to the heavier equipment (*le gros outillage*).
12	B	This question requires you to consider a **number and combination** of options and the only way is to **consider each one in turn**. The relevant points are in the second half of the second paragraph beginning with *La raison première est économique* which is given as the first reason in the options. The second is in the next two sentences *Les femmes s'y collent* (= literally they are 'stuck with it') and *… elles sont aussi nombreuses à vivre seules* (just as many women live alone). Option 3 and 4 are plausible but not accurate enough for the original, so that the correct answer is Options 1 and 2 only.

Key points to remember

- You are **not expected to be a specialist** AS or A level language student, but the expected minimum standard is a Grade C at GCSE and that you will have made some effort to keep up your knowledge after GCSE. Expect to know **between 30 and 70%** of the answers to the questions.

- Practise skills of **reading for gist, skimming and scanning**, in order to **identify main points**. Often the answers are to be found **in the title or sub-title** and **at the beginning and end of paragraphs**.

- Use the **vocabulary lists**. They give words needed to answer the questions that you will may not have come across at GCSE.

- Look for **appropriate material for practice** in such sources as *Paris Match, L'Express, Le Nouvel Observateur, Die Welt, Der Spiegel, Stern, Bildzeitung, El Pais, El Mundo* and the French, German and Spanish versions of *Authentik* and *Étincelle*, which are specialist publications for GCSE and A level language students in schools and colleges.

- You have approximately **45 minutes to answer 25 questions**, which means you can spend only about seven or eight minutes on each extract – three minutes reading the extract and one minute per question.

- Remember the advice about tackling multiple-choice questions given in *Do Brilliantly AS General Studies*.

Remember that often answers can be found in the titles and the first and last sentences of paragraphs.

HOROSCOPE LUNAIRE
Quelles surprises vous réserve la Lune en juin?

A **Bélier (21 mars–20 avril)**

Du début du mois et jusqu'au 12 juin environ, Vénus vous boudera, et cela provoquera quelques petites tensions avec votre cercle familial, amical ou sentimental. Mais la nouvelle lune du 13 balaiera tous ces petits tracas et vous replongera dans le monde de la communication, des échanges et des rencontres …

B **Gémeaux (21 mai–21 juin)**

Votre légèreté agira sur vous comme des bulles de champagne, surtout en ce mois anniversaire! Mais, attention, cette boisson est à consommer avec modération … Trop sûr de vous, vous risquez de trop vouloir provoquer les choses.

C **Vierge (23 aout–22 septembre)**

Après un ralentissement dans vos affaires ou dans vos études, et encore quelques petits tracas jusqu'à la nouvelle lune du 13 juin, ça va cartonner! Quant à la pleine lune du 28, elle vous fera décoller, destination succès. Rien ne vous arrêtera! Vénus étant votre complice, vous serez heureux en amour et vous aurez une progression au top du top!

D **Balance (23 septembre–22 octobre)**

Copains et copines, en route pour la fiesta! Eh oui, Mercure, planète de la communication, vous dit d'établir le contact n'importe comment, avec n'importe qui, mais toujours avec le sourire. Du charme, une certaine jeunesse d'esprit et de l'humour, voici un mois ou vous vous éclaterez à fond! Pas question de perdre votre sérieux, tout simplement d'être plus cool...

Vocabulary

tracas	problems, worries
cartonner	to move, pick up
complice	ally
balayer	to sweep away
s'éclater à fond	to have a ball

Under which sign, **A** to **D**, are people told to expect

1   a favourable love life?

2   friction within the family?

3   that they could be too self-confident?

4   a lot of socialising?

SANTÉ: TATOUAGE ET PIERCING: *attention, prudence*

La mode du tatouage et du piercing connait un succès fou. Mais attention de ne pas faire n'importe quoi. Ne considérez pas que le tatouage ne présente aucun risque. Bien entendu, la technique est rôdée et si toutes les conditions d'hygiène sont réunies, il n'y aura aucun problème (sauf certains cas d'allergies). Soyez tout de même prudent. Tous les tatoueurs ne sont pas forcément scrupuleux sur les questions d'asepsie (désinfection). Beaucoup ont des stérilisateurs peu efficaces. Adressez-vous à des gens reconnus qui vous garantissent d'indéniables conditions d'hygiène. Les aiguilles à utiliser doivent avoir un usage unique.

Il faut savoir que les détatouages laissent des cicatrices et des brûlures peu esthétiques. Seuls les lasers de type Q-Switched permettent de faire disparaître les pigments sans brûler la peau. Mais ces appareils sont rares en France, leur utilisation délicate, le nombre de séances important et leur coût élevé.

D'abord l'hygiène

Avec le piercing, les principaux problèmes rencontrés surviennent quand la personne se perce seule. De plus en plus de jeunes le font eux-mêmes, ce qui est très vivement déconseillé, car les risques sont vraiment réels. Dans ce cas, il faut consulter immédiatement un médecin. Autre conseil: ne jamais s'échanger les bijoux ou autres 'prothèses'. À vrai dire, l'hygiène doit rester la principale préoccupation de celui ou celle qui se fait percer. Assurez-vous que le perceur vous garantisse toutes les conditions de propreté (aiguille à usage unique …). Privilégiez les parties facilement accessibles à la toilette. Le nez ou la langue sont des éléments plus fragiles (donc des zones à risques). Évitez les matériaux qui s'oxydent comme l'acier chromé. Il est préférable (même si c'est un peu plus cher) de porter de l'or ou de l'acier chirurgical.

En conclusion, soyez vigilant si vous souhaitez être tatoué ou percé. Les risques d'infection bactérienne sont importants, de même que ceux de transmission des virus du sida et de l'hépatite B.

Vocabulary			
rôdé	refined, perfected	*toilette*	washing
asepsie	sterilisation	*s'oxyder*	to rust
aiguille	needle	*acier*	steel
propreté	cleanliness, hygiene		

5 The article states that the most important factor in tattooing and piercing is the

A skill and experience of the artist

B method of sterilisation used

C risk of an allergic reaction

D use of the latest technology

6 The greatest hazard with body piercing among young people is

  A using old or used jewellery

  B the risk of bleeding

  C the use of infected needles

  D doing it yourself

7 Which two metals are recommended for use in body piercing?

  A gold and surgical steel

  B gold and silver

  C gold and chrome

  D gold and platinum

8 According to the passage, which of the following statements is **not** true?

  A There is a risk of contracting AIDS and Hepatitis B

  B It is recommended that only disposable needles are used

  C Standards of hygiene vary between practitioners

  D The problems are likely to affect only young people

COMBINE SNCF: LES VOYAGEURS FANTÔMES AVAIENT TOUS LE MÊME COIFFEUR

Il se faisait rembourser les places achetées par téléphone avec les numéros de Carte bleue de ses clients.

Après les voyageurs sans billet, les billets sans voyageurs. Des dizaines de Parisiens se plaignaient de voir leur compte débité par Carte bleue du prix d'un billet de train qu'ils n'avaient jamais acheté. Casse-tête pour la SNCF qui porte plainte à son tour. La police étudie les relevés de compte: tous ces voyageurs fantômes n'ont qu'un point commun, ils ont le même coiffeur, avenue Marceau. C'est la clé de l'énigme.

Un employé licencié de ce salon de coiffure, Frank G., avait fait un double de la clé; la nuit, il y retournait clandestinement pour inventorier les facturettes Carte bleue de la caisse. Il notait les numéros dont il se servait ensuite pour réserver des places de train par téléphone ou Minitel. Puis il passait prendre le billet à la gare et se le faisait rembourser en liquide au guichet où il expliquait qu'il avait raté son train. Ce tour de passe-passe lui a rapporté 80 000 F et un aller simple au palais de justice. Ce qui ne résout rien pour les victimes de l'escroquerie: à la SNCF, les trains partent à l'heure et on ne rembourse pas deux fois le même billet.

Vocabulary			
combine	scam	*licencié*	dismissed
casse-tête	puzzle	*se servir de*	to use
porte plainte	file a complaint	*tour de passe-passe*	sleight of hand
relevés de compte	bank statements		

9   A number of Parisians complained to the police about

   A   delayed train journeys

   B   misuse of their credit card accounts

   C   the price of train journeys

   D   trains not running

10   Frank G. worked

   A   at a hairdressing salon

   B   as a night clerk

   C   as a police detective

   D   at a credit card company

11   The first stage of the scam was taking

   A   credit cards from customers

   B   credit card slips from the till

   C   cash from ticket offices

   D   credit card numbers over the telephone

12   Then he would

   A   go and buy train tickets

   B   credit his own account through Minitel

   C   claim a refund for unused tickets

   D   sell tickets for cash

13   SNCF refuse to reimburse

   A   single tickets

   B   tickets reserved by phone

   C   tickets reserved by Minitel

   D   the same tickets twice

Answers can be found on pages 103–104.

2 MECHANICAL AND SPATIAL RELATIONS

In A2 General Studies the testing of mechanical and spatial relations is specific to **AQA Specification A**. It tests your understanding of the principles that govern the way in which simple tools, machines and devices work, and your ability to visualise interactions between two and three dimensions. This is problem solving with the emphasis on skills of analysis, synthesis and logical reasoning. The test appears as the first of two questions in **Unit 5 (Science, Mathematics and Technology)** where the second is an essay (**one** from a choice of six questions). In the test there will be a mix of scenarios, typically two sets of mechanical and two sets of spatial problems, each consisting of about seven or eight multiple choice questions, with an overall total of 20–25 questions. The example questions given here are typical of a range of different problems. For more examples you should look at some past papers.

QUESTIONS AND ANSWERS

For each of the questions, choose the answer you consider the best of the alternatives **A**, **B**, **C** and **D**.

THREE-DIMENSIONAL PERCEPTION

1 Which of the following types of two-dimensional drawings does **not** provide any information about the height of the corresponding three-dimensional object?

A contour   **B** net   **C** plan   **D** elevation

2 Three of the cubes labelled **A** to **D** are identical. All four have six different faces. Which cube is not the same as the others?

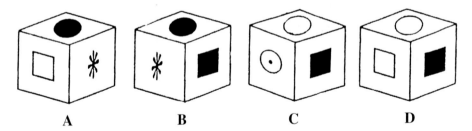

    A   **B**   **C**   **D**

3 Consider the three nets below. Which of them can be folded to form a tetrahedron?

 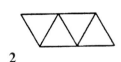

  1   **2**   **3**

Answer
  A **1** alone is correct
  B **1** and **2** only are correct
  C **1** and **3** only are correct
  D **2** and **3** only are correct

4

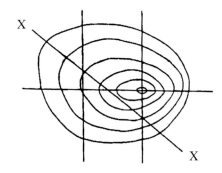

The diagram above shows the contoured map of a hill and the four straight lines indicate the position of the four sections shown below. Which section (**A** to **D**) corresponds to the line marked **XX** on the contour map?

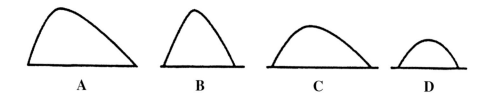

A   **B**   **C**   **D**

5 The isometric drawing below shows wooden blocks stacked in uniform layers on a horizontal surface.

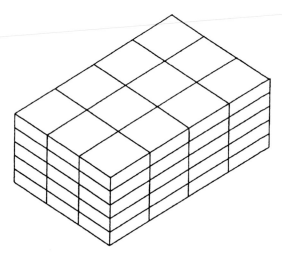

The number of blocks where exactly one face is not touching another face is

A 11

B 18

C 22

D 26

6 In the pulley system shown below three points labelled P, Q and R have been marked on the strings.

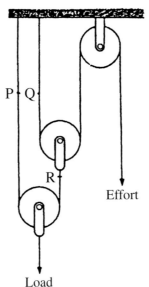

How do these points move when the string marked 'effort' is pulled downwards?

A P moves upwards   Q moves upwards   R moves upwards
B P moves upwards   Q is stationary   R moves upwards
C P is stationary   Q moves upwards   R is stationary
D P is stationary   Q is stationary   R moves upwards

7 The six pulley wheels in the system shown below have been labelled P, Q, R, S, T and U.

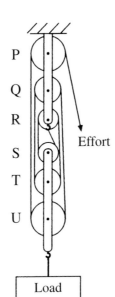

When the string labelled 'effort' is pulled downwards to raise the load, what is the motion of the wheels when viewed as shown?

A All six wheels move anti-clockwise
B All six wheels move clockwise
C P, Q and R move clockwise; S, T and U move anti-clockwise
D P, R and T move clockwise; Q, S and U move anti-clockwise

LEVERS

Study paragraphs 1 to 4 and Figures 1 to 3 below on the subject of Levers and then answer the questions that follow.

(1) Since time immemorial mankind has struggled to lift heavy objects, such as large building stones, and over the years, various devices have been introduced to make such tasks easier. The simplest device is probably a lever, which is used in three different ways.

(2) Figure 1a shows a Class 1 lever where the pivot or fulcrum, marked F, lies between the load to be lifted and the effort applied to the other end of the lever. Figure 1b is a schematic diagram of the forces applied by the load at L and the effort at E. The force needed at E is less than that needed to lift the load directly, provided F is closer to L than to E.

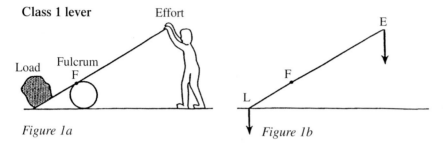

Figure 1a   Figure 1b

(3) Figures 2a and 2b show a Class 2 lever where the fulcrum is at one end, the effort is applied to the other end and the load is between them. In this case the effort needed is always less than that to lift the load directly, as F is always closer to L than to E.

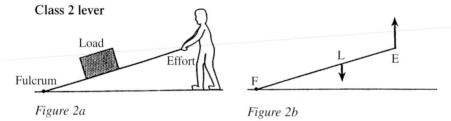

Figure 2a   Figure 2b

(4) Occasionally a Class 3 type of lever is used where the effort is applied between the fulcrum and the load (Figure 3). In this case the effort is always greater than the load.

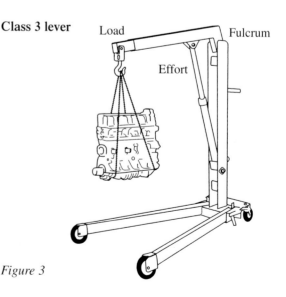

Figure 3

8 The two diagrams below show a storekeeper loading an oil drum onto a trolley and then wheeling it away.

 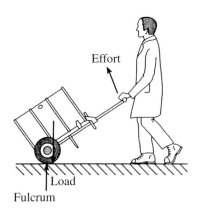

The types of lever shown in use in the two situations are
A initially Class 1 and then Class 1
B initially Class 1 and then Class 2
C initially Class 1 and then Class 3
D initially Class 2 and then Class 2

9 The diagrams below show various tools or instruments involving levers.

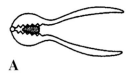 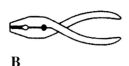 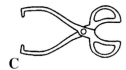 

A   **B**   **C**   **D**

Which involves a Class 3 lever?
A nutcrackers
B pliers
C tongs
D tweezers

10 The route up an inclined plane that will require the greatest force to push or pull the same object in each case is:

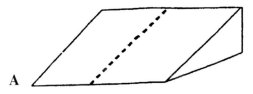 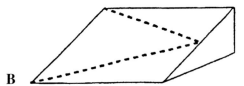

A   B

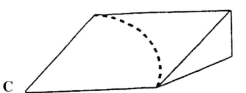 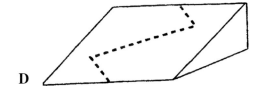

C   D

How to score full marks

Question	Correct answer	Examiner's hints
1	C	You need to be familiar with terms like these – they are **basic technical terms** used in the context of maps, geometrical drawings, plans, elevations and the like. Contours are lines drawn on a map usually to show the height of land above sea level. A net is a two-dimensional shape that can be folded to make a three-dimensional shape. A plan in this context is a top- or over-view of a structure drawn on a horizontal plane, e.g. a floor plan. An elevation is designed to show the vertical dimensions or height of a structure. Therefore it is the plan that does not show the height of an object.
2	D	One way to solve this is to **construct a net** initially showing that A and B **could be** identical. The view of C can then be obtained from this net. The blank square and shaded square on opposite faces of the cube in A, B and C mean that D is unobtainable, so has to be the **odd one out**.
3	B	The most **efficient and logical** way to do this is to visualise **1** with the three outside triangles folded upwards to make a four-sided object (tetrahedron). So option **D cannot be correct**, meaning that either **2** or **3** do not make a tetrahedron. Net **2** will also fold to be a tetrahedron (as it is a variation of **1**) but **3** will not. The correct answer is therefore **1** and **2**.
4	C	Options A and B **may be discounted** because they both show the highest point and the line XX does not pass through the highest point. XX is therefore the wider of the two sections C and D.
5	C	You have to be absolutely precise in interpreting the wording of the question here. How many blocks are there with **exactly one** and **only one** face not touching another? These are the ones shaded below facing outwards in the centre of each side of the block. You can see 11 of these in the drawing, which means that there is another 11 on the other two sides, producing 22 in total.

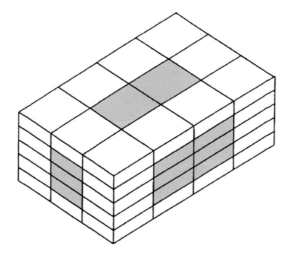

Question	Correct answer	Examiner's hints
6	D	If you **analyse the process** and the relative positions of P, Q and R you should be able to work out that, **initially**, R moves upwards (ruling out **C**) but P and Q do not, which leads immediately to answer **D**.
7	B	First of all, P moves clockwise, which **excludes A**. U must also move clockwise which **excludes C** and **D**. So the correct answer **has to be B** – all the wheels move in the same clockwise direction. It pays to be **thoroughly logical** in your approach.
8	B	If you **match the patterns** showing the **relationship between Effort (E), Load (L) and Fulcrum (F)** in the introduction with those in the question, you can see clearly that the first action involves EFL (Class 1) lever and the second action ELF (Class 2) lever. A **mnemonic** for remembering the types of lever in order is 'EFL the ELF FEL'.
9	D	Using **the same principles**, the nutcracker A is ELF (Class 2); the pliers B and tongs C are EFLs (Class 1); and the pair of tweezers D is the only FEL (Class 3) occurrence.
10	A	The weight component of the object acting down the plane will be a maximum when the **angle of the plane** is a maximum. Therefore **A** will require the greatest force.

Key points to remember

- The basic standard of scientific and technical knowledge expected for these questions is GCSE Grade C in Double Award Science. Any extra technical or scientific knowledge needed for individual questions is given with the material.

- It is essential to appreciate the way levers, gears and pulleys play their part in many mechanical applications, how they work individually and in conjunction with each other.

- You must also have plenty of practice at working with, and translating between, two- and three-dimensional representations, e.g. mirrors, reflections, plans and elevations, and understanding the principles behind perspective and photography, contours and cross-sections, as in the Questions to Try (e.g. the closer the contours the steeper the incline, etc).

- Good sources for practice are maps, weather charts, geometrical or technical drawings, building plans, descriptions and demonstrations of how things work, assembly instructions or manuals. There are also many appropriate books, encyclopaedias, CD ROMS and web sites you can consult.

- You have approximately **45 minutes to answer 25 questions,** which means you can spend only about ten minutes on each of the four sections – four to five minutes studying the extract and one minute per question.

- You should also follow the general guidance about how to approach multiple-choice tests given in *Do Brilliantly AS General Studies*.

1 The cube below has been formed from which net?

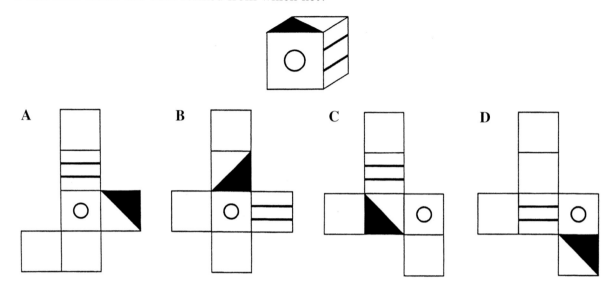

2 If opposite faces of each dice below total seven and the dice are identical, what is the sum of the numbers on the four faces that are placed together?

A 9
B 11
C 14
D 16

3 The two elevations shown below correspond to which set of contours?

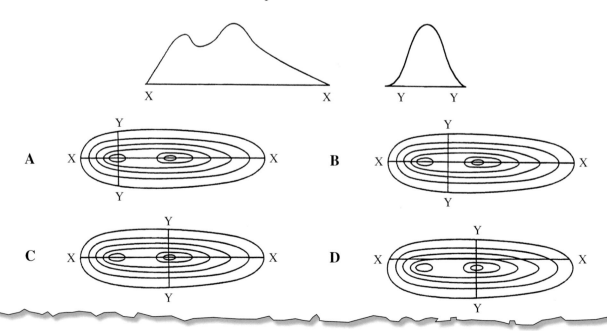

4 Which of the hill elevations corresponds to the contour map?

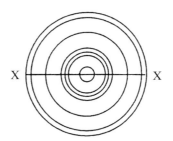

A 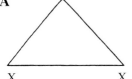 B 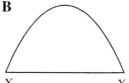 C 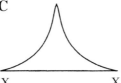 D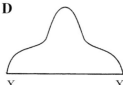

5 The following isometric drawing is symmetrical and made from 20 cubes. The shaded areas represent empty spaces.

The number of cubes with three non-touching faces only is

A 8
B 12
C 16
D 20

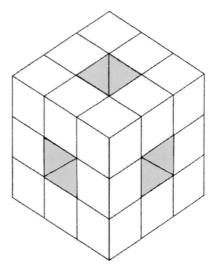

6 A shadow of a person is cast on the frosted glass of an office door by light from a desk lamp inside the office. An observer outside the office notices a change in the shadow, as indicated in the diagram below moving from left to right.

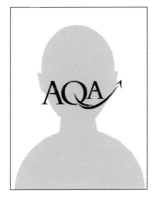

The most likely explanation for the change is that

A the observer has moved further away from the door
B the observer has moved nearer to the door
C the person inside has moved nearer to the lamp
D the person inside has moved further away from the lamp.

GEARS

Study the figures and information below on the subject of gears and then answer the questions that follow.

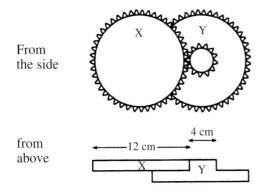

For every one rotation of gear X, gear Y rotates three times.

The gear ratio of the train is 3 : 1 (Diameter of X : Diameter of Y)

Figure 1 A gear train of two gears

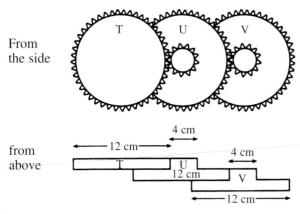

For every rotation of gear T, gear U rotates three times and gear V rotates nine times.

The gear ratio of the train is 9 : 1

Figure 2 A gear train of three gears

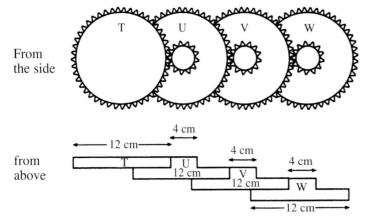

Figure 3 A gear train of four gears

The questions refer to Figure 3.

7   The gear ratio of the train is
    A 3 : 1
    B 9 : 1
    C 27 : 1
    D 81 : 1

8   If the speed of rotation of gear U is 20 revolutions per minute (rpm), the speed of gear W will be
    A 20 rpm
    B 60 rpm
    C 180 rpm
    D 360 rpm

9   The number of rotations of gear T needed to make gear V turn 144 times is
    A 8
    B 16
    C 32
    D 64

10

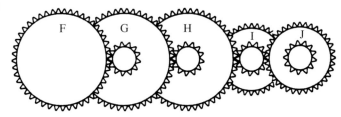

Figure 4 A gear train of five gears

In Figure 4 if gear H is rotating clockwise then
A All gears are rotating clockwise
B F is rotating anti-clockwise
C F and J are rotating anti-clockwise
D G and I are rotating anti-clockwise

Answers can be found on page 104.

ANSWERS TO QUESTIONS TO TRY

These model answers would score full marks, so you can compare them against your own. We have provided comments on why the answers are particularly good.

PART A Using sources

1 Identifying and commenting on the main points (pages 11–12)

🎯 How to score full marks

(a)   The main aims of the Government's proposals are 'to reform and rebalance the criminal justice system to deliver justice' and 'to safeguard the interests of victims, witnesses and communities'.

(b)   Four of the measures planned are:
  (i)   A Bill to tackle anti-social behaviour. This is designed to make it easier to deal with such problems as anti-social tenants, graffiti, fly tipping, vandalism and the disruption they cause to local communities.
  (ii)   A Bill to reform sentencing arrangements and criminal procedures. New types of sentence will be introduced to protect the public from dangerous offenders and retrials will be allowed for those acquitted of serious offences where new and compelling evidence emerges.
  (iii)   Legislation to reform the courts system. Magistrates' Courts and the Crown Court will be brought together to work more effectively and efficiently under a single organisation.
  (iv)   A Bill to modernise the laws on sexual offences and penalties for offenders. This will crackdown on paedophiles using the Internet and will strengthen the notification requirements of the Sex Offenders' Register.

> **Examiner's comments**
>
> This answer does exactly what the questions require – no more, no less in each case – and it would score full marks. The broad aims of the Government's proposals are set out at the **end of the first paragraph** and in **each subsequent bullet point** the bills described are the measures intended to bring these aims about. In each case there is a **brief explanation of what the changes in legislation are intended to do**. Similar comments made about **the last two bullet points** would score equally with the others chosen in the model answer.

2 Analysing and commenting on data (page 16)

🎯 How to score full marks

(a)   (i)   Number of female prisoners in 1994 = $0.037 \times 48\,794 = 1805$
    Number of female prisoners in 2001 = $0.058 \times 67\,054 = 3889$
    Increase in number of female prisoners between 1994 and 2001 = 2084
  (ii)   Number of male prisoners in 1994 = $48\,794 - 1805 = 46\,989$
    Number of male prisoners in 2001 = $67\,054 - 3889 = 63\,165$
    Increase in number of male prisoners = $63\,165 - 46\,989 = 16\,176$
    Percentage increase in number of male prisoners = $16\,176/46\,989 \times 100 = 34.42\%$

(b)   The increases in the prison population could be explained by a number of possible factors:
  • changes in sentencing policy, such as: more custodial sentences, increasing the length of sentences, reducing the eligibility for remission/early release
  • increases in serious crime and improved detection rates
  • increased use of detention for prisoners on remand or for non-criminal prisoners such as illegal immigrants
  • the greater involvement of females in serious or repeated crime, particularly drug-related offences.

3 Analysing and summarising key points from data (pages 22–24)

How to score full marks

The charts and information show that the world's energy resources are unevenly distributed and the geography of energy production and consumption is highly uneven.

Chart 1 in particular shows that three countries, the USA, Russian Federation and China, dominate both the production and consumption of energy. Chart 2 shows that some countries, typically the oil-exporting states, such as in the Middle East, West Africa, South and Central America produce much more than they consume. Many of the most advanced industrial economies, such as the USA, Central and Western Europe and Japan, consume vastly more energy than they produce. The USA is the largest single energy consumer, using over a quarter of the world's energy despite having only 5 per cent of its population.

Chart 3 shows that nearly two thirds of proven oil reserves are concentrated in the Middle East, proven reserves of natural gas are dominated by the former Soviet Union and the Middle East, while coal reserves are more evenly distributed between the Asia-Pacific region, North America and the former Soviet Union.

The text information indicates that the world's consumption of primary energy is increasing all the time and supplies of oil and natural gas are finite and due to run out during the 21st century. Alternative renewable energy sources are relatively under-exploited despite some increase in their use.

The main implications are that the high energy consumers, such as the USA, Japan and Europe, are reliant on continuing imports and access to relatively cheap resources from other countries to supply their economies, and that the energy exporting countries have a position of some power over both price and supply of oil and gas in particular. This represents a source of tension and friction between the West and Middle Eastern countries.

The rich countries are also reluctant to place limits on growth, despite concerns about environmental pollution and global warming, for fear of damaging their economies. They tend to use their economic and military power to exert economic and political pressure on poorer countries to continue to supply their needs.

The longer-term implications are that alternative, renewable, less polluting and more sustainable energy sources will have to be developed by the richer nations, preferably sooner rather than later, to avoid economic and environmental chaos in the not too distant future.

There is an element of **Assessment Objective 4** in the question (3 out of the 9 marks), in this case for recognising the **implications of the data and text**. The response is able to meet this requirement well by showing good awareness of the economic, political, environmental and technological tensions and uncertainties which exist between the production, consumption and trade in energy at an international level.

4 Analysing knowledge and arguments (pages 31–33)

How to score full marks

(a) **Objective assertions**

… studies of the genome are now revealing how our chances of suffering from more common illness, such as diabetes, Alzheimer's, heart disease and asthma, also depend on our DNA. (lines 21–23)

It is illegal in the UK to alter the genetic make-up of sperm and eggs. (lines 69–70)

Subjective assertions

Most people are uncomfortable with the notion that access to good health should depend on your ability to afford it. (lines 36–37)

The science of genomics has a great deal to offer society, and should spark a revolution in medicine and healthcare. (lines 73–74)

(b) The difficulty with the argument in Dexter and May's article is that it is based largely on speculation and uncertainty about the impact of the solving of the human genetic code. It is difficult to disagree with their final conclusion that there is a need for more dialogue to ensure that this new knowledge is properly applied and that the 'wonderful' opportunity (line 79) is put to good use, but this is based on the argument throughout that there are lots of questions which need answers. And so it is a kind of circular argument.

The article makes use of lots of rhetorical questions and the trouble with this approach is that the answers are not supplied. Sometimes they may be implied, as in the question in lines 37–38 'Would you be happy to see the benefits … made available only to a wealthy few?' The implied answer is no, but this itself is based on the subjective assertion immediately preceding it that 'most people … are uncomfortable with the notion that access to good health should depend on your ability to afford it'. This may be true, but no evidence is supplied to support it.

There are other arguments in the article which are not supported, such as the claim that that 'healthcare based on genomics is likely to save us money' (line 57). This is based on the statement in the lines that follow that 'at present, most of medicine is focused on the relatively expensive business of treating the symptoms of an illness'. This may or may not be true, and possibly could be justified, but it is not here and therefore the claim is not fully justified.

The other difficulty with rhetorical questions is that they can be answered in more than one way, and therefore may confuse rather than develop the argument. Why are the questions about insurance in lines 45–52 'contentious', for example? The reasons for this claim and those that follow are not explained, as if they are self-evident.

Perhaps the authors are right and these are genuinely difficult questions that cannot be left to scientists and policy-makers alone. Perhaps society does need to find a consensus, but in the end the authors force us to take it at face value that there are so many questions that need answers.

Examiner's comments

This is a difficult question that needs a careful answer because, in a number of respects, the article is well-written, articulate and persuasive, and yet you are required to criticise it. For this reason you have to look very precisely at the arguments being put forward to analyse exactly **what types of knowledge and**

arguments are used, and where **genuine justification** is provided. These skills are useful for all General Studies questions testing AO4 but for **Edexcel** candidates in particular you have to understand the terminology and the purpose of the examination question very clearly. You should **avoid giving your own view, unless you are invited to give it**, and just concentrate on the wording of the question and analysing the case being presented.

5 Analysing knowledge and arguments, Assessing validity and value of a source (pages 38–39)

How to score full marks

Simon Jenkins' article is an entertaining piece of journalism lamenting the problems he has experienced with having to convert to new Windows software in his work as a journalist. It is possible for the reader to sympathise with his difficulties and dissatisfaction, particularly if it all worked perfectly well before, as he claims. However he goes on to use his own experience of developments in IT to attack the education and communication skills of young people and it is not clear to me what his evidence is based on.

His main attack on writing skills starts in the paragraph which quotes Dr Johnson ('What is written without effort …'). The argument here seems contradictory. He claims that the slowness of handwriting disciplines the brain and that the facility of the computer leads to sloppiness. This however is not consistent with his earlier claim that the computer encourages you to rewrite several times over. Presumably the reason for this would be to improve the quality of the expression, which I would argue is the opposite of sloppiness.

He then goes on to attack e-mails, and although he does find some merit in the increase in lovers' letters, he says that words printed on a screen are 'emotionally ponderous … monotonous' … and 'their meaning becomes distorted in transmission'. What does he mean by this? He seems to think that printed words lack the care and character of handwriting. If composed in haste maybe, but then handwriting can be done in haste as well (as I am having to do in this exam) and very few people these days use 'glorious copperplate', except my grandad. But then my grandad cannot use a computer either.

He also quotes politicians who regularly complain about standards in the 'three Rs', but only really mean reading and arithmetic, implying that no-one these days cares about writing. Where is the evidence for this? The fact is that more and more attention is being paid to literacy, including 'joined-up writing', as well as numeracy, in the government's education policy. I use a computer at home and at school, but I still handwrite essays and most exams are handwritten. So you still need to be able to write, and as far as I know, handwriting is extensively taught at primary school alongside computer skills. It is probably true that it doesn't have the same prominence now as it did before computers came along, so I agree with Mr Jenkins to that extent, but when I think of all the benefits of computers, like access to information and many other resources via the Internet, rather than the negatives which he has chosen to gripe about, just like my dad, I think that these days young people have more extensive and useful skills than just copperplate handwriting.

Examiner's comments

This candidate has given a neat and well-argued rebuttal of Simon Jenkins and deserves full marks. Not all candidates would have the confidence to do this but the personal references are very effective in response to the author's and are just as authentic and valid. This is another 'to what extent …' question which allows you to go in the direction you like, but note that the candidate always seeks to provide reasons for their point view, both in criticising Simon Jenkins (usually on grounds of lack of evidence) and in explaining and justifying their disagreement. There are also points where the candidate acknowledges agreement and this adds to the impression the examiner gets of careful and balanced evaluation of the passage and the author's views.

6 Summarising and evaluating key issues in a source (pages 44–45)

🎯 How to score full marks

The opening paragraph of Source A is a clear indication of the growing importance of what is often called 'grey power'. Retirement is taken earlier and many over 50s have more money to support their more varied leisure interests. Improved diets and medical advances have improved the quality of life for older people and they form an increasingly influential lobby with their votes to cast and money to spend. Politicians and retailers acknowledge the importance of grey power and the fact that older people are more aware of their rights – although perhaps not usually in the sense of Margaret Simey's assertive call for 'more outrage'.

Source B makes clear the potential for medical science to lengthen life spans and statisticians have revealed the extent to which older people form an increasingly higher proportion of the population. Elizabeth Taylor and Julie Andrews are both famous film stars who, though of pensionable age, still have an aura of glamour although their lifestyles have been very different. Source C offers just a few examples of how activities like rock climbing and teaching IT – not usually associated with older people – can be part of their increasingly diverse lifestyles.

Scientific projects like William the worm and Dolly the sheep create a sense of amusement but the results of this research may have profound implications. The nematode worm project might help in the fight against crippling, debilitating and often life-threatening diseases and mental illnesses. Cloning is another, much publicised, possibility although there are many scientific and ethical issues to be resolved before this is more widely used.

It is important, though, to offer a balanced picture of the life of older people. There is still no legislation to prevent age discrimination and there are many people who lack the family and community support of Pushpa Chaudhary. Old age might also bring decreased mobility and social isolation. It is important to emphasise the point made in Source C that the quality of life for older people is at least in part determined by a measure of financial security.

My own community reflects some of the contrasts and is perhaps typical of parts of northern England. Major industries have disappeared and wages are lower than the national average. Rows of terraced houses have disappeared over the years and this has broken up close-knit communities, often of extended families. Illness rates are higher, especially for heart and lung complaints, and a high proportion of people exist – there is no other word to describe their lifestyle – on disability allowance.

There is a minimum income guarantee for those able to fill in the forms or who do not let pride get in the way of claiming it. Politicians are good at building up hopes and making promises but these are often not realised. This can lead to apathy and a feeling that things were better in the 'old days' – times when doors were left unlocked and assaults on old people were rare.

Things have changed. There is more sheltered housing and, for those who have the mobility, cheap bus fares and reduced prices at entertainment and leisure places run by the city council. Shops have a lot more to offer and there are plenty of cheap holidays including some very exotic locations.

There is life beyond bingo and more opportunities to get involved. Not everyone wants to take it. Old beliefs and values do not change rapidly but for those who do, there are plenty of possibilities. It is not unusual to see older people learning about computers and even, like the former editor of *The Guardian*, teaching a few tricks to their grandchildren. For those with a decent pension and who have that most valuable thing, their health, life can be far less harsh and unrelenting than in the 'good old days'.

It is unwise to generalise because communities vary – mine is less affluent than many – and so do personal circumstances and the sources help to illustrate this. There are old people who are lonely, worn out and desperately poor. There are others who see the 'third age' as an opportunity to try out new things, some of which might be both energetic and adventurous. I am part of the latter, a mature student at the city's FE college. After A levels, I hope to study for a degree. My 'economic situation' is bearable. I am even not as afraid of 'outrage' as I used to be. Trying to be as objective as I can in a situation where the heart can rule the head, I am still aware that the statistics offer a very inconclusive picture about the world of grey power, monster medicine and the geriatric ward.

> **Examiner's comments**
>
> Only in the final paragraph did this candidate reveal her rather unusual personal circumstances. She could be allowed a **measure of subjectivity** at the end because what came before it was **objective analysis** of a very high quality which showed her ability to do all the things required by the Assessment Objectives and, in particular, AO3. The first half of the answer used the source material in a very intelligent way, adding support where required, but not doing it excessively. The second half gave a very clear picture of a changing community but, in formulating her conclusions, the candidate showed the extent to which circumstances can vary, even in one community. Behind the statistics there are the individual cases, which form part of our personal experience and help to shape our own beliefs and values. This candidate showed the rare ability to **remain objective without de-personalising** the content of her essay. It is a skill that examiners will reward fully.

PART B Essay questions

1 Short essay answers (page 49)

How to score full marks

1   It is impossible to provide an exhaustive list of the principles that might be used to identify the quality of a work of art because tastes vary and so many factors could be used. Dali's surrealism might be judged on its bold, striking and shocking images. Impressionists like Monet use colour and technique to blur reality and soothe the senses. The Angel of the North has line, design and the qualities of creative engineering. Unmade beds and sheep in formaldehyde are deemed by some to be imaginative. Time will tell and the test of time, like monetary worth, is one of the hallmarks of aesthetic evaluation.

> **Examiner's comments**
>
> This was a well-written and knowledgeable answer. Four or more aesthetic principles were identified – each gaining a mark to a maximum of 4.

2   Much may depend on the political stance taken and the papers read. Being 'tough on crime' is a vote winner. The prison population in the UK has been rising for years and is now almost the highest, per head, in Europe. Most people want to see serious criminals – murderers, rapists and major drugs dealers – locked up for a long time (at the very least). A bigger problem is that of the petty criminals and habitual minor re-offenders. While they are in prison they can't break into houses or commit other crimes. People feel more secure. It is widely believed that those who commit a crime should be punished, if necessary by being deprived of their liberty for a while. Unfortunately, prisons are full of drugs and low-life crime tutors.

The extract shows a more positive side – rehabilitation through education and temporary release schemes. The law is not clear on whether 'the punishment fits the crime' (either for the criminal or the victim) except in the case of mandatory life sentences in cases like murder. Otherwise, judges interpret the law and use their sentencing powers in different ways. Perhaps there should be no remission but that would leave little incentive for reform and good behaviour. If the punishment does fit the crime – an elusive and ill-defined claim – it would be prudent to put more resources into preparing prisoners for life on the 'outside'. Fewer re-offenders might allow more concentration on trying to determine if the sort of punishments we have really do fit the crime. As the extract is from *The Guardian*, perhaps someone should ask Erwin James who writes an informative Thursday column for the paper. He's serving a life sentence.

2 Long essay answers (page 56)

How to score full marks

1 It is not true that the whole of Britain is among the windiest areas in Europe, but particularly in more exposed westerly areas, conditions are ideal for generating electricity from wind turbines. (The greatest concentrations – 44% of the 960 turbines in the UK – are in Wales and proposals to extend wind-generation schemes are often controversial.)

The blades of wind turbines are essential to the process of generating electricity because they turn a gear mechanism, which is attached to a generator. The power output is directly proportional to the cube of wind velocity. Large blades are more efficient and, commercially, wind farms need to be located in areas where the average annual wind speed is greater than 5.5 ms^{-1}. It is necessary to space out the turbines to prevent a reduction in wind speeds in the central part of the wind farm, so large areas of land are required.

To counter environmental objections, off-shore floating platforms could exploit the wind more fully. However, it should be noted that wind farms operate for only one third of the time because of variations in the wind speed and there may be no generation on the sort of cold winter mornings when demand is highest.

Those in favour of the further development of wind farms emphasise that their development would reduce dependency on non-renewable fossil fuels. No fuel is used in the process and there are no harmful emissions or wastes beyond the manufacture and disposal process. Indeed, significant savings could be made on the consumption of coal with comparable reductions in the emission of carbon dioxide and sulphur dioxide. The installation of wind turbines would be unlikely to conflict with farming operations in the areas concerned and, in view of the precarious economic plight of many farmers (particularly hill farmers), wind turbines would inject much-needed money into the rural economy. The British Wind Energy Association even claims that wind farms are a tourist attraction in their own right.

Opponents of wind farms argue that they are visually intrusive and that they present dangers to birds because of the rotating blades – a point emphasised by the RSPB. The 'swishing sound' made by the blades and the hum of the generator may produce localised noise pollution and it is claimed that the turbines contribute to television and radio interference in the areas concerned. In terms of health and safety, wind farms placed close to a road may distract drivers and the blades can present a danger if they become detached. Because their use depends so heavily on weather-related variables, critics dismiss wind turbines as inefficient. Both planners and ecologists point to the possible conflicts that might arise owing to the large area of land required – for example, national park authorities are opposed to the siting of wind farms within their boundaries.

There is an element of romance about old-style windmills, which are often seen as desirable architectural features and they offer a vision of rural Britain which is fondly remembered by older people. Modern turbines can be 400 feet high because height helps to generate more electricity and the contemporary white towers do not blend easily into the environment. The target of generating 20% of the UK's electricity through on-shore wind farms has major implications for land use and the landscape. Clearly, most electricity will continue to be generated using finite fossil fuels but the technology associated with wind power as renewable energy is already proven. The balance between short- and long-term energy generation needs and the wider aspects of environmental protection will not easily be achieved.

Examiner's comments

This was a **knowledgeable** and **intelligently written** answer. It spotted that the question was **in two parts** and answers the first by showing clear **scientific knowledge** and **understanding**. The second part of the answer was equally successful with the **analysis** used as a vehicle for a detailed consideration of both the **benefits** and **disadvantages** of using wind turbines to generate electricity with a technical understanding that was accessible **to the general reader.** It provided **informed, balanced discussion** incorporating the **latest thinking** on off-shore wind generation and the conclusion, highlighting the balance between commercial needs and environmental protection followed **logically** from the previous arguments.

---

3 Report writing/problem solving exercises (pages 62–63)

⦿ How to score full marks

1 **(a)** Stated simply, the problem is a disagreement between miners at Tower Colliery and managers over instructions given to two miners to change their work schedule. Coalface workers refused to be transferred to another part of the pit when the work schedule was changed and miners on the morning shift walked out in sympathy.

This strike did not have the support of the NUM who tried to persuade the afternoon shift to work normally. Despite this, these men also decided to strike. Communication between those involved in the dispute appeared to be poor and there was no facility to resolve the dispute as there had been under British Coal. Ironically, the situation was one in which the miners were effectively striking against themselves.

Before the establishment of a workers' co-operative five years ago, Tower Colliery had a reputation for militancy and elements of the culture of worker solidarity may still prevail. A director of the co-operative, Tyrone O'Sullivan, has stated that this is the first industrial dispute since the take-over and that the two men concerned had refused to do a job that they were trained to do.

Mr O'Sullivan has stated that production has now stopped. In an area of high unemployment and widespread social deprivation, a sustained stoppage could have profound effects both for the workers personally and on a local economy where there is little economic diversification. Even in a co-operative, someone must have the managerial capacity to make strategic decisions.

(b) It is a cliché to say that there are two sides to every story, but industrial disputes are often marked by the capacity of the two sides involved to recognise only their own point of view. As an independent consultant, my job is to identify areas of common ground, which may serve to bring the sides together. This is even more important in an organisation that describes itself as a 'co-operative'.

There is a long history of solidarity in collieries such as Tower. The unity of the miners has always been important in determining the outcome of industrial disputes. Nevertheless, managers need to be able to take an overview and it is their job to manage the deployment of the miners at Tower. The two men who refused to accept the transfer to another part of the pit, where they would be doing a job for which they have been trained, have effectively brought production to a standstill. The strike has no official backing from the NUM. There is a local culture of solidarity but this sympathy strike threatens the livelihoods of all employed at Tower. Competition in selling coal is fierce.

However, it is also necessary to look closely at the way in which the decision was made. Management by instruction often reduces co-operation and can promote a divisive 'them and us' situation. The co-operative need to know more about the work record of the two men involved and to ask whether this was an isolated issue. Some measure of job rotation may not be unreasonable but consultation – perhaps involving the NUM – might help to reduce possible suspicion and unease. Transfer without adequate warning could have practical implications for the men concerned and these need to be taken into account.

Tyrone O'Sullivan has inferred that this is the first dispute in the five-year history of the co-operative. Apportioning blame, especially, if all the facts have not been fully investigated will not secure the resumption of production. It is that which will safeguard jobs and help to protect the interests of a co-operative venture that contributes up to £10 million a year to the local economy.

(c) The main recommendations to minimise a risk of recurrence are:
- A co-operative council should be established on a formal basis. This will contain representatives of the NUM, workplace representatives and management.
- Roles and responsibilities of all groups should be made clear. The overriding principle should be that of co-operation. This may involve elements of workplace training and clarification of the role of the NUM.
- A mechanism should exist, which is understood by all, to establish procedures that might be used to resolve a dispute before strike action is taken.
- There needs to be wider recognition that co-operatives need to work as a team not as competing groups. This may necessitate a review and possible revision of existing contracts of employment.
- The importance of cultures and sub-cultures in closely-knit mining villages which are experiencing levels of profound social and economic change need to be more widely understood. The values of the workplace need to be understood in a wider context.
- New managers, with greater experience of consultative management methods, could be an asset to the co-operative.
- It may be that the co-operative would benefit from a more detailed report drawn up after further study of the problem by an independent consultancy, preferably with experience of production methods and labour relations in traditional heavy industries.

It should be emphasised that the selection of isolated recommendations is unlikely to prove effective. Conditions in 2002 reflect profound and fundamental changes that have taken place in the mining industry in the last 20 years. The size of the industry, its workforce and the position of the NUM have declined significantly in that period – to the extent that most coal is now imported and very few indigenous pits survive.

Co-operatives are an expression of an ideal but, as the report indicates, cultures are slow to change and working relationships between 'workers' and 'managers' can be uneasy. Change breeds insecurity, frustration and industrial unrest. Those concerned need to understand what is required of them and this is where a clear training programme is important.

Striking should always be the last resort because, in many respects, it is a recognition of failure. The alternatives are stark. Many miners in South Wales and other parts of the country have either not found alternative employment or are in jobs which offer low pay for limited skills. Solidarity needs to extend not just to the workplace, but to the locality where the spending power of working miners is important, indeed vital.

> **Examiner's comments**
> (a) An **effective start** helps to provide the candidate with **confidence** and helps to show the examiner that the person writing has the **skills** to meet the Assessment Objectives. This part of the answer **highlighted** the problems of the dispute and was particularly effective in contrasting the **long-** and **short-term** impact.
> (b) The opening paragraph was very important because it dealt with the difference between **objectivity** and **subjectivity**. As an 'independent

consultant' the writer showed the importance of recognising that **one-sided** reports fall a long way short of their function and that relatively small disputes often have **wider** and more **complex causes** and **consequences.**

(c) **Bullet points** are not usually advisable in more traditional essays but, in this part of the report, they are **used effectively** to make the recommendations **clear.** The more **extended writing** in the latter part of the answer shows a **detailed** and **balanced** grasp of the key issues, again helping to give a **wider context** to disputes in an industry where the loss of jobs has had severe effects on life in **mining communities. Communication skills** were outstanding throughout the report.

The answer is presented very effectively, using the separate sections, in a **report format** and this is important in the context of what is required by this style of question in AQA Unit 4 Specification B.

4 Essays based on sources (pages 68–70)

How to score full marks

Direct action is not always the first method that pressure groups use. It is wise not to generalise about pressure groups because there are so many in existence. Some, such as the RSPCA and the NSPCC are well-known and have been established for a long time. They are better funded than most and usually have 'insider' status which means they are drawn into the more respectable machinery of politics at Westminster. Their direct action is rarely of the type that breaks the law but their tactics can be effective in other ways, such as some powerful and eye-catching advertising.

The source used in this question uses examples of direct action often associated with 'outsider groups' campaigning *for* animal rights and *against* what they see as unjustifiable experiments carried out by major research organisations such as Huntingdon Life Sciences – prime 'baddies' in the eye of some animal rights activists.

Justifying direct action is not necessarily very difficult. Ideally, all disputes should be settled calmly and rationally, leading to a consensus. This is the civil service ideal for insiders where everyone understands the 'rules' and works within the law. Changes are rarely dramatic or rapid. Those excluded from the process may feel that they have little power or influence. They may have tried peaceful forms of direct action like writing letters to MPs or marching peacefully. Such tactics are easily justified in a democracy that allows freedom of speech.

Animal rights protestors are often young and sometimes impatient. They may be seeking publicity for what they see as their cause. These are people who may argue that humans do not have the right to 'exploit' animals and, as the source shows, HLS has itself broken the law through its treatment of puppies. Defenders of HLS – indeed many people in society – might argue that research by 'higher order' humans on animals is not justified for cosmetic purposes but that it is necessary and therefore acceptable, under humane conditions, for some types of medical research.

Most manufacturers of cosmetics now state that their products are not tested on animals. This is partly because of the work of pressure groups, but it is impossible to identify which groups and how much each might have contributed. For some, perhaps those who are members of the British Union for the Abolition of Vivisection or the Animal Liberation Front, this is not enough. Often their action is more direct, such as harassing shareholders like David Braybrook, or becoming shareholders of companies so that they can ask awkward questions at annual company meetings.

In a sense, the issues brought out by the source suggest a wider struggle – against 'big business' and 'capitalism', or the cold and clinical detachment of the scientists involved in experiments on animals. Tony Juniper of Friends of the Earth, an environmental pressure group, refers to this as 'turning faceless people into individuals'. It has, though, led to accusations of 'economic terrorism' with calls for the government to take severe action against the environmental and animal rights 'terrorists'.

This raises legal issues and to some extent resolving them is clear. Those who break the law should expect to be dealt with according to the law. Some protests against HLS staff have been violent and dangerous. In such circumstances it is extremely difficult to make an argument for breaking the law. Ideally, it would be easy to say that laws must never be broken.

It is more difficult to separate the law from morality. Sometimes laws need to be challenged because, no matter what the original intentions were, the laws do not have widespread support. There were protests in the 1980s against the poll tax and many were far from peaceful. Eventually, such pressure led to a change in the law. David Braybrook seeks to defend his liberty but so do Reclaim the Streets who are mentioned in the source. Protest is not necessarily 'wrong' but nor is breaking the law 'right'. If laws were routinely broken there would still be a sort of freedom – based on anarchy.

It is often said that one person's terrorist is another person's freedom fighter and this helps to highlight the dilemma. Individuals can, if they wish, devise their own moral codes in which disagreement is recognised through tolerance of the views and beliefs of someone else. The law is something that can help to safeguard our freedom. It has to be applied universally and not on a 'pick and mix' basis. Scientific researchers have a legal right to conduct their activities without being terrorised by those who are breaking the law.

Finally, it should not be forgotten that politics is often about power, and power is unevenly distributed. Boards of directors and those who are influential in the City are powerful and may not act in a way that supports the public good. Dissent and peaceful protest are essential rights which we should seek to safeguard but violence to other people and, perhaps to a lesser extent in the scale of values, to property, is much more difficult to justify. Life-saving drugs have often been developed as a result of tissue research based on animals. The saving of human life, to most people, probably represents a greater good but not everyone will necessarily agree.

The law should help to protect our liberty. Those who break the law, or abuse their freedom – be they researchers, financiers or protestors – may have to accept the consequences of their actions. Ultimately, in circumstances free from violence, it may be necessary to break the law to protect its integrity. In a system that is not always representative of the interests of all, direct action can never be ruled out entirely as an option.

Examiner's comments

One of the outstanding qualities of this essay was its ability to **integrate** material from the source **into the answer,** thus avoiding a common tendency to copy out source material in an uncritical way. The opening paragraphs use both **examples** and **concepts.** Instead of condemning direct action, the writer shows that **some forms of direct action are lawful.**

Another strength of the essay is its ability to take a more **strategic view** of pressure group activity without losing sight of the **source.** This is crucial when answering a **synoptic question** and allows the writer to show a **wider perspective,** bringing together elements of **economic, social, legal and scientific** issues.

Equally impressive was the way in which **AO4 marks** were gained in sections where comparisons were made between **law** and **morality** and the extent to which knowledge may be **interpreted differently.** The **analysis** is sophisticated but clear; the difficult issue of the extent to which **breaking the law** might be **justified** is clearly addressed and there is an interesting, almost **enigmatic twist,** to the **conclusion.**

🎯 How to score full marks

Question	Correct answer	Examiner's hints
1	C	The answer is to be found in the **last sentence** of *Vierge. Vénus étant votre complice, vous serez heureux en amour* (Venus is the Goddess of Love and the text says she will be your accomplice and you will be happy in love).
2	A	This is in the **first sentence** of *Bélier. Vénus vous boudera* (will have nothing to do with you), *et cela provoquera quelques petites tensions avec votre cercle familial …* (and this will cause some tensions within your family circle).
3	B	Here the answer is very clearly in the **last sentence** of *Gémeaux. Trop sûr de vous* (Over-confident), *vous risquez …*
4	D	The **first sentence** of *Balance* and process of elimination give you this in *Copains et copines* (boyfriends and girlfriends), *en route pour la fiesta!* (head for the party!) and later with *vous vous éclaterez à fond!* (you will have a ball! – given in the vocabulary).
5	B	This questions tests your understanding of the key point in the first paragraph, which says that tattooing is popular, but risky; the technique is well tried, but hygiene is highlighted as the most important factor. The **last three sentences** of the paragraph all concern the need for sterile conditions (*les questions d'asepsie* – also given in the vocabulary) and the need for hygiene continues to be emphasised in the remainder of the article.
6	D	The clues here are in the **first and second sentences** of the third paragraph *Avec le piercing, les principaux problèmes rencontrés surviennent* (the major problems arise) *quand la personne se perce seule. De plus en plus de jeunes* (More and more young people) *le font eux-mêmes …* (both talk about 'doing it on your own/by yourself').
7	A	The answer is clearly stated in the **last sentence** of the third paragraph *Il est préférable (même si c'est un peu plus cher) de porter de l'or ou de l'acier chirurgical* (= It is preferable, even if a little dearer, to use gold or surgical steel – once again given in the vocabulary).
8	D	Option A is mentioned in the **last sentence** … *de même que ceux (les risques) de transmission des virus du sida* (AIDS) *et de l'hépatite B.* Option B is mentioned twice in *aiguille(s) à usage unique* at the end of the first and middle of the third paragraphs. Option C is also covered in the middle of the first paragraph with *Tous les tatooeurs ne sont pas forcément scrupuleux sur les questions d'asepsie (désinfection).* Although much mention is made of young people in the article, it clearly is not solely about them, which rules out Option D and means it is the correct answer. Take care to spot a negative in a question.
9	B	The article is about a credit card (*Carte blue*) scam involving a hairdresser and unused train tickets. The specific references which make B the correct answer are in the **sub-title** and the **second sentence** *Des dizaines de Parisiens se plaignaient de voir leur compte débité …* (Dozens of Parisians complained about their accounts being debited).
10	A	At the **beginning of the second paragraph** it says *Un employé licencié de ce salon de coiffure, Frank G …* (a former employee of the hairdressing salon).
11	B	The same sentence goes on to say *avait fait un double de la clé* (had a duplicate made of the salon key); *la nuit, il y retournait clandestinement pour inventorier les facturettes Carte bleue de la caisse* (at night he returned in secret to make a list of the credit card slips from the till).

12	C	Then the article goes on to explain *Puis il passait prendre le billet à la gare et se le faisait rembourser en liquide au guichet où il expliquait qu'il avait raté son train* (Then he took the ticket to the station and exchanged it for cash at the ticket office where he explained that he had missed his train).
13	D	The answer here is in the very **last sentence** *à la SNCF, les trains partent à l'heure et on ne rembourse pas deux fois le même billet* (at the SNCF, trains leave on time and they do not reimburse the same ticket twice).

2 Mechanical and spatial relations (pages 88–91)

🎯 How to score full marks

Question	Correct answer	Examiner's hints
1	D	Notice that the black triangle on the top face **must be adjacent** to the face with the circle. This **rules out** options A and C. The white triangle on the top face must be adjacent to the face with the two parallel lines, which **only happens** with D.
2	B	As the opposite faces of each dice total 7, the left dice **must have** 3 facing the middle dice. The right dice must have 6 on its (hidden) right-hand face, as it is the left dice turned anti-clockwise through 90 degrees. Therefore the right dice has 1 facing the middle dice. This is **as far as you need to go** as the two opposite faces of the middle dice must total 7. (Actually by turning the middle dice clockwise through 90 degrees the hidden numbers must be 6 on the right and therefore 1 on the left.) Whatever, this gives a sum of $3 + 7 + 1 = 11$.
3	C	Here YY passes through the highest point, so this **excludes** A or B. D would not show a pair of humps as it misses the centre of the hill and the highest points and only 'peaks' in one place. **By elimination** and also because XX 'contours' the centre of the hill, showing two high points and the second higher than the first, the answer is C.
4	D	Walking across XX to the centre of the hill would be characterised by steep/shallow/steep/shallow rises and the **only pattern that fits** this is D.
5	A	The only cubes that have **three non-touching faces only** are the corner pieces and there are eight of these. All others have four non-touching faces.
6	C	A and B may be **excluded** because the observer's position has no effect on the situation inside the office. **A sketch** should convince you that moving nearer to the lamp leads to a bigger shadow on the frosted window in the door.
7	C	This is straightforward if you follow and **apply logically** the progression in the introduction on gears. In the train of two gears the ratio is $12 : 4 = 3 : 1$. In the train of three gears it is $9 (= 3 \times 3) : 1$. In the train of four gears in Figure 3 therefore for one turn of T, there will be $3 \times 3 \times 3 (= 27)$ turns of W.
8	C	First **remove T** from Figure 3. One turn of U will result in 9 turns of W, so a speed of 20 rpm for U will result in a speed of 180 rpm. (A slower way of course is to multiply U by 3 for V, and V by 3 for W.)
9	B	This question requires an **inverse approach** to the previous one which means that when V has turned 144 times, T will have turned $144 \div 9 = 16$ times.
10	D	You should know that connected gears turn in **opposite** directions, so if H is turning clockwise then G and I are both turning anti-clockwise, which is option D and the **only pattern** of those given that will work.